Mushrooms

A Grayscale Adult Coloring Book

40 Coloring Pages

Copyright © 2018 Tania Heady
All Rights Reserved.

No part of this publication may be reproduced in any form or by an electronic or mechanical means, including information storage and retrieval systems, without permission in writing from the copyright owner.

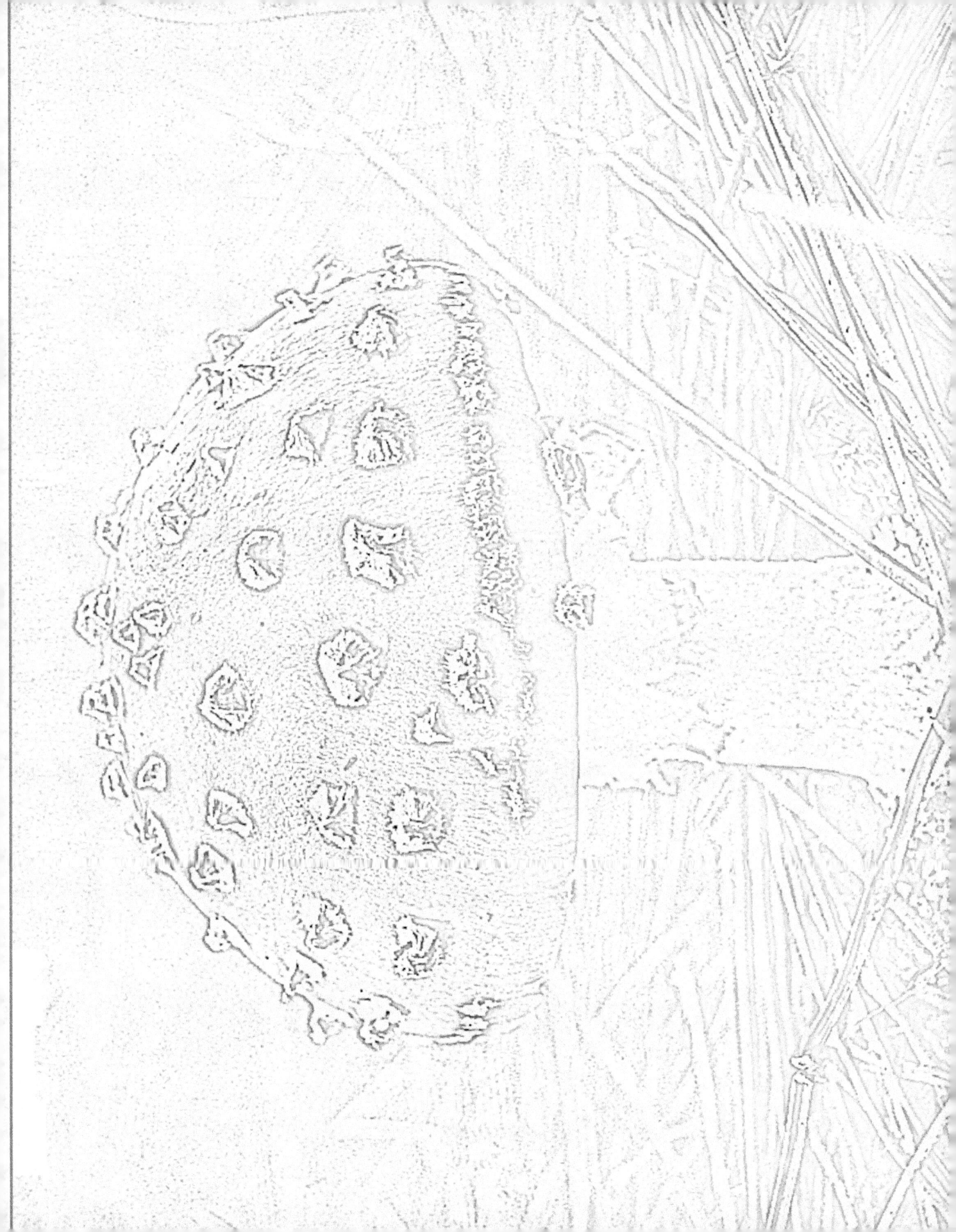

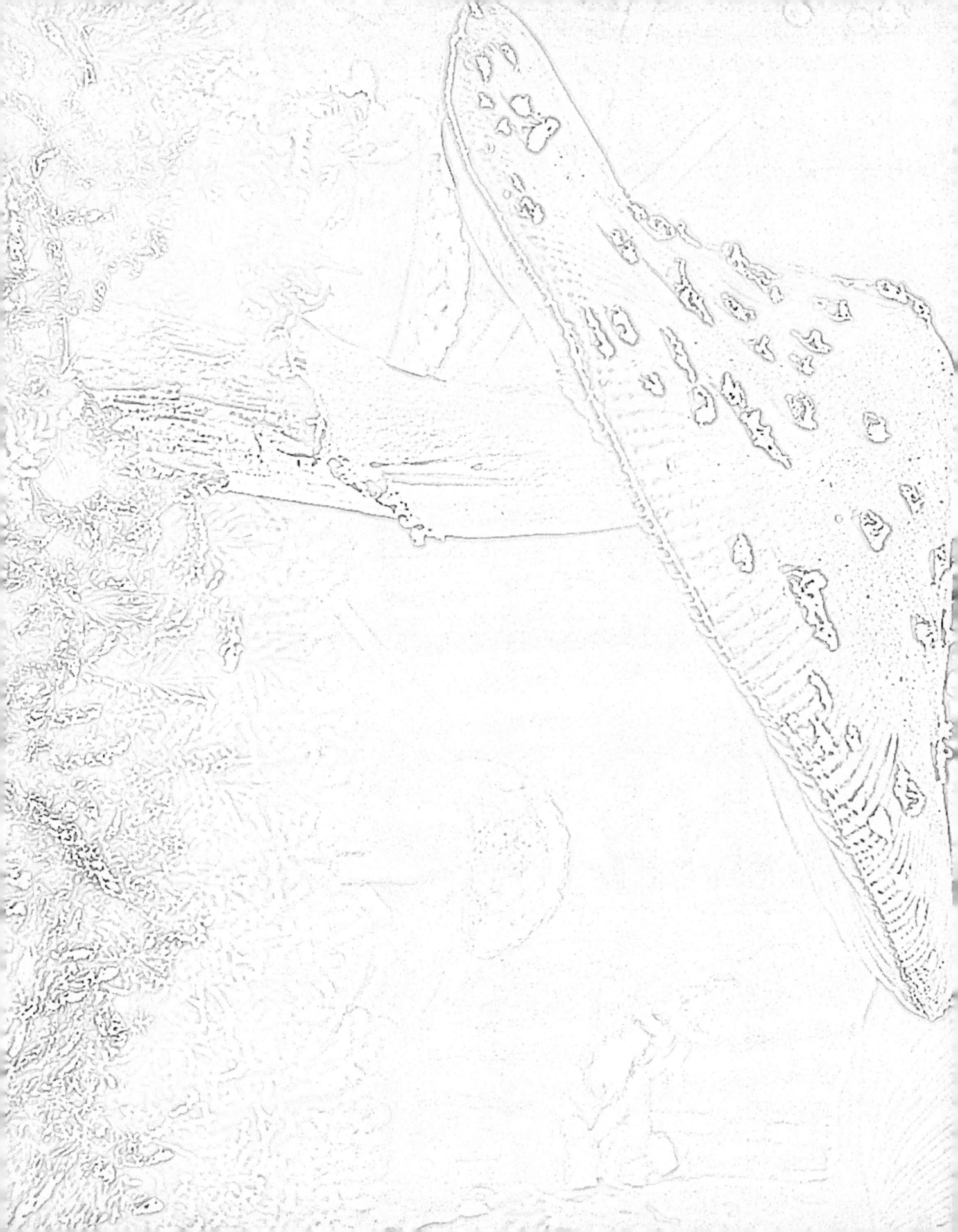

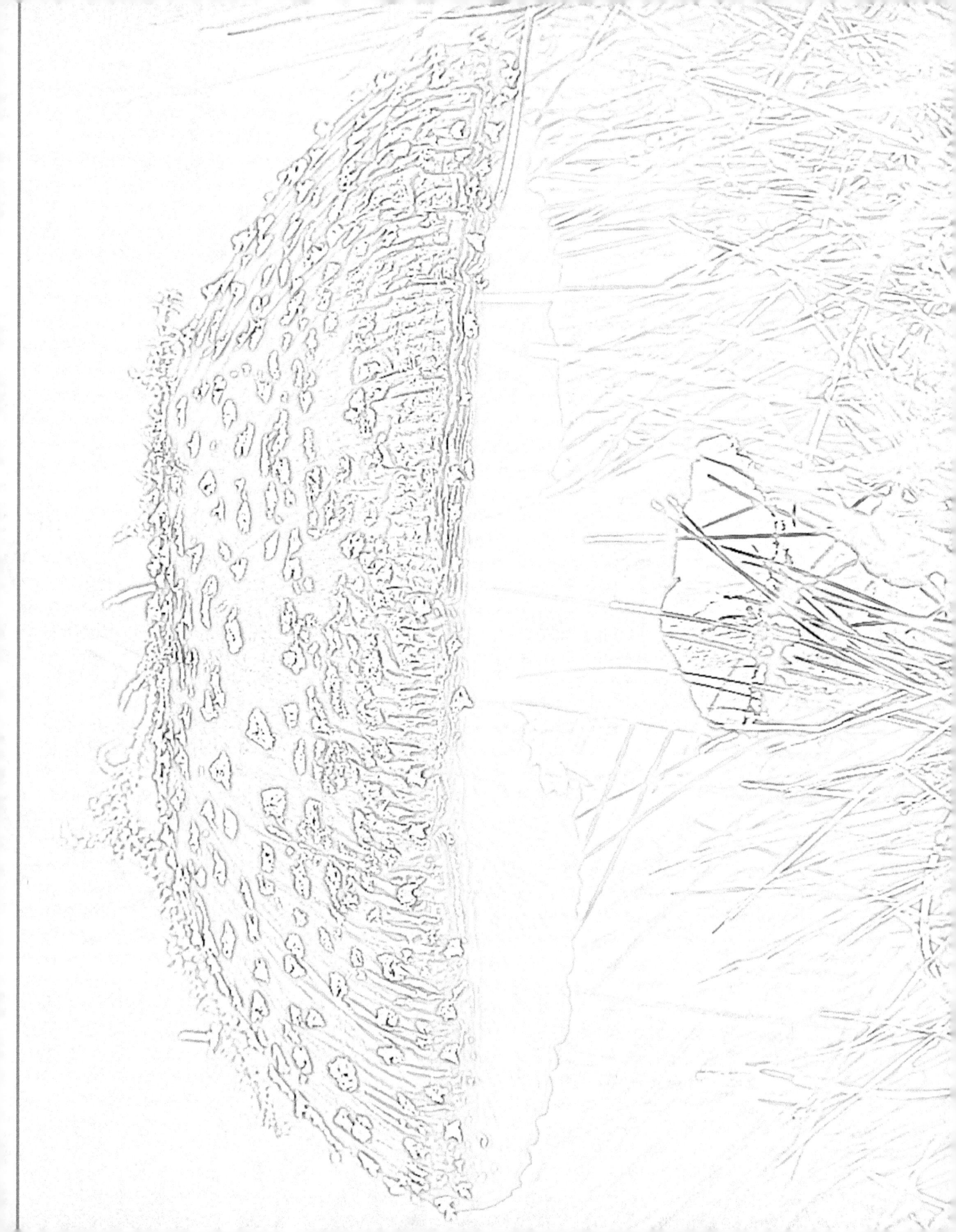

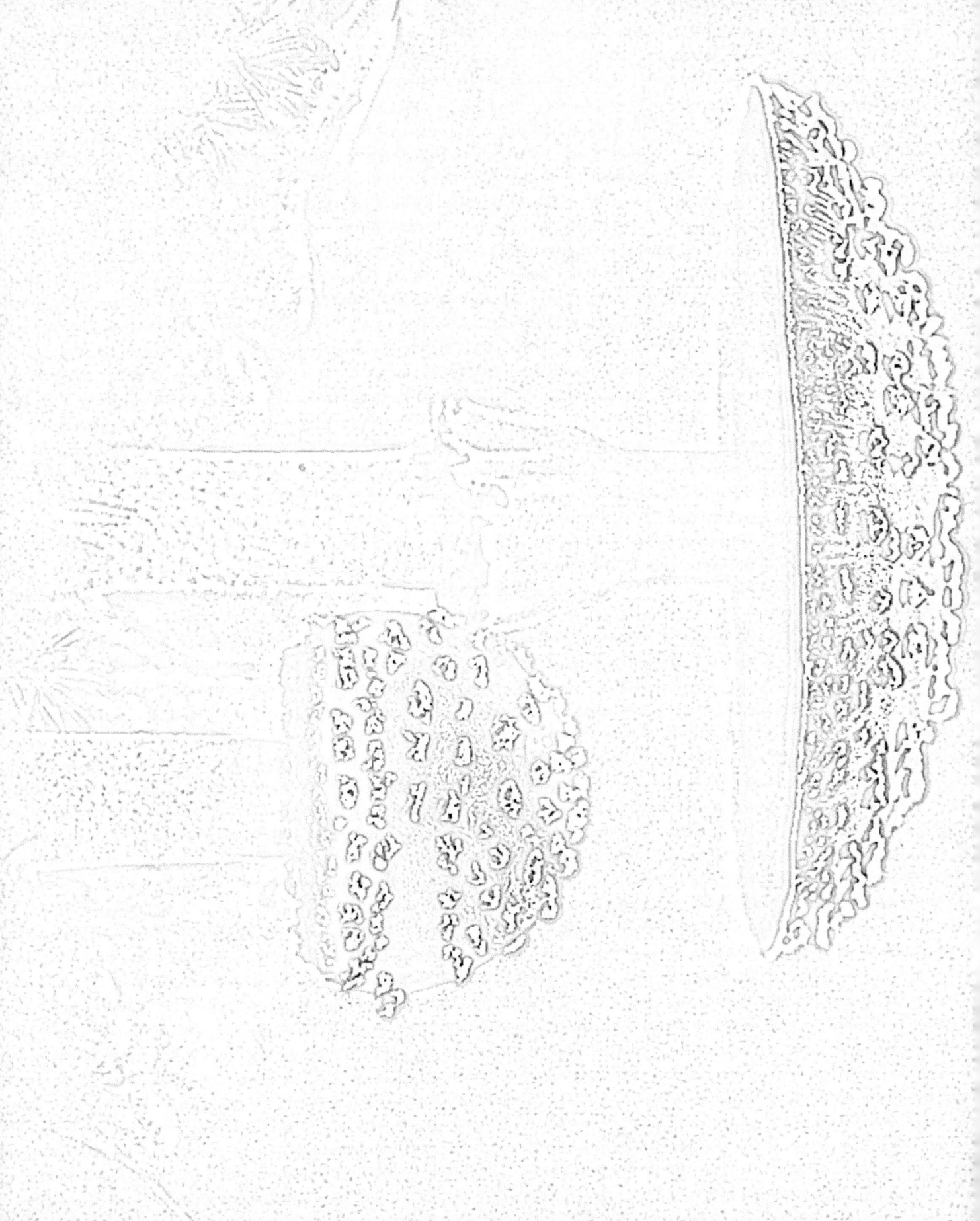

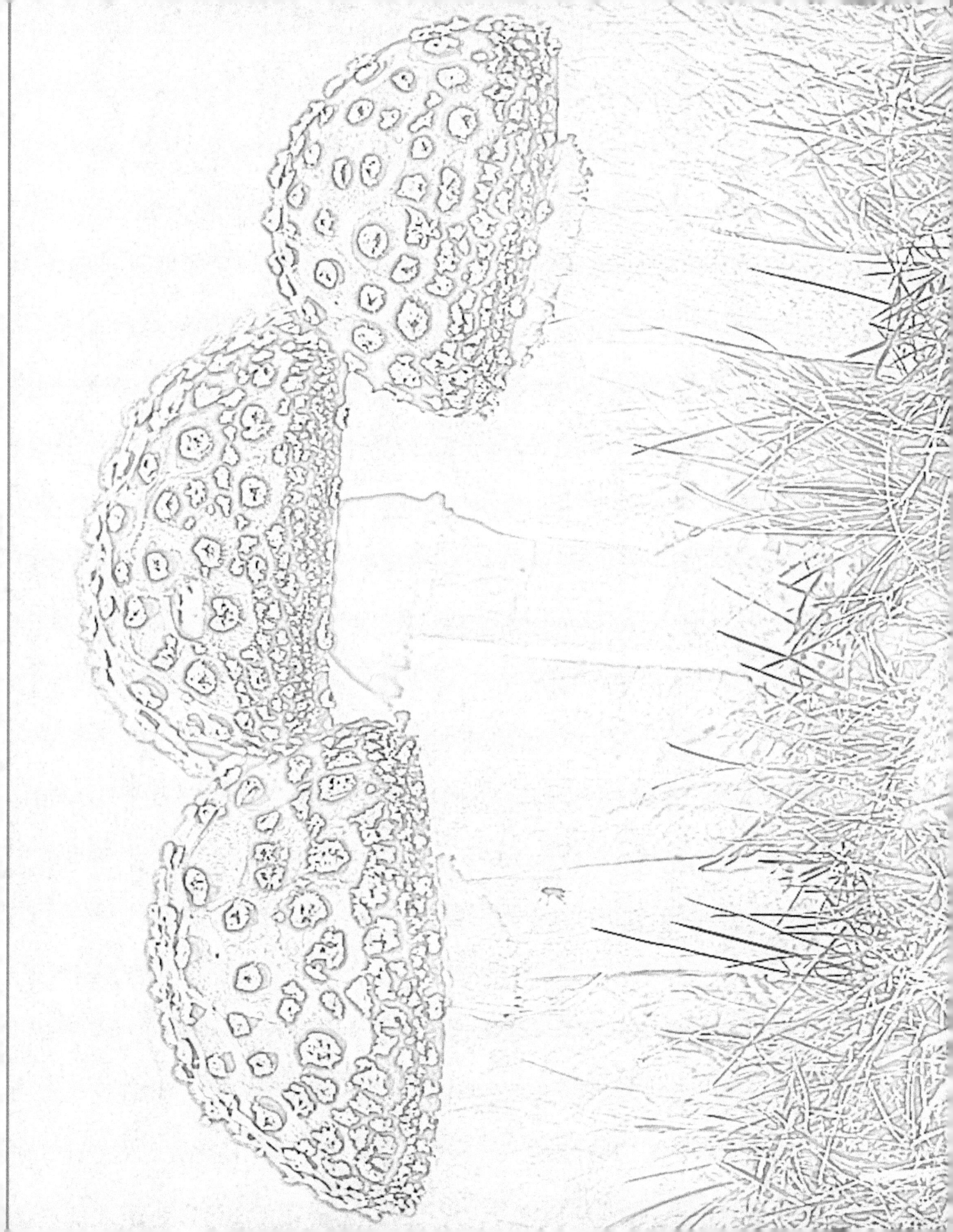

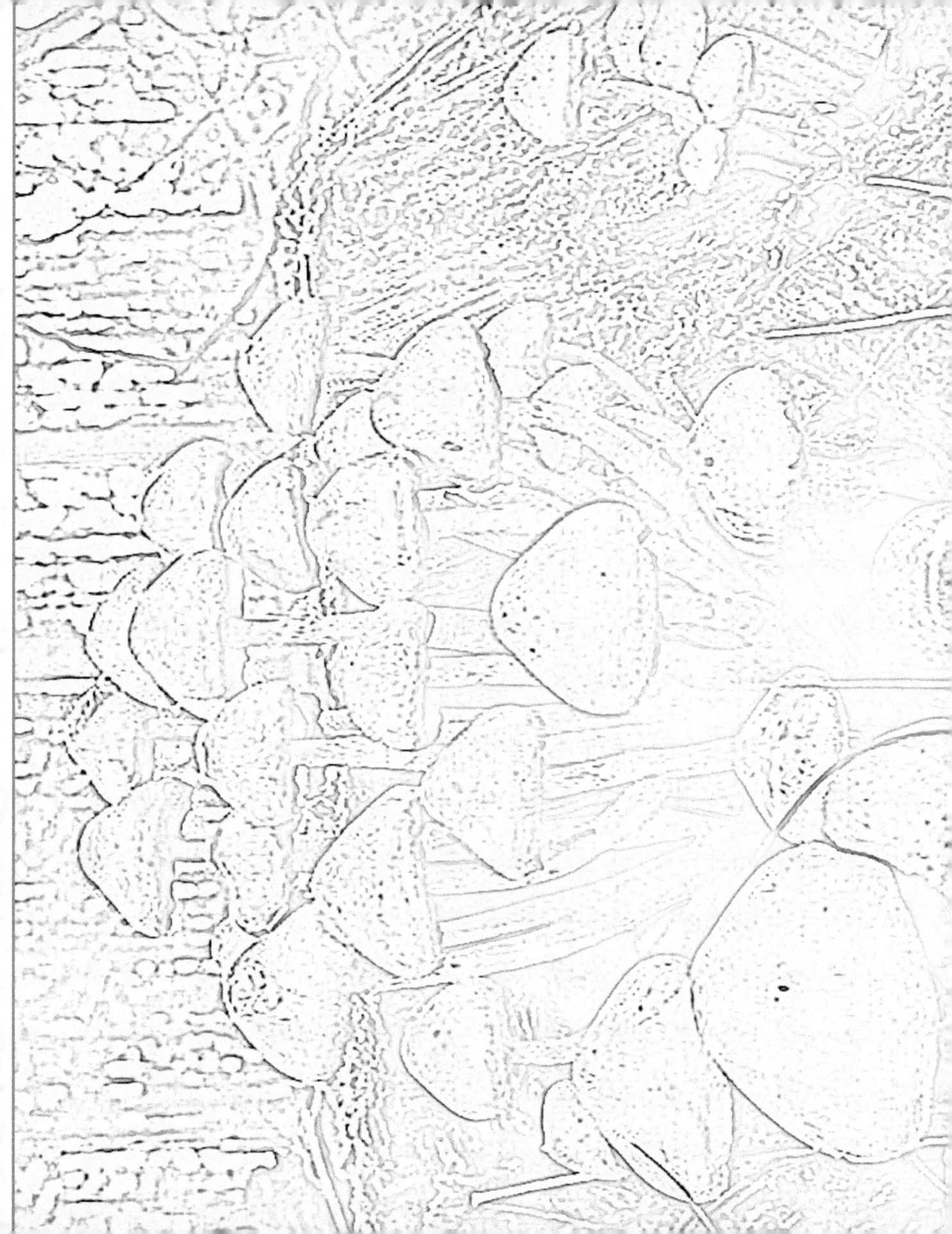

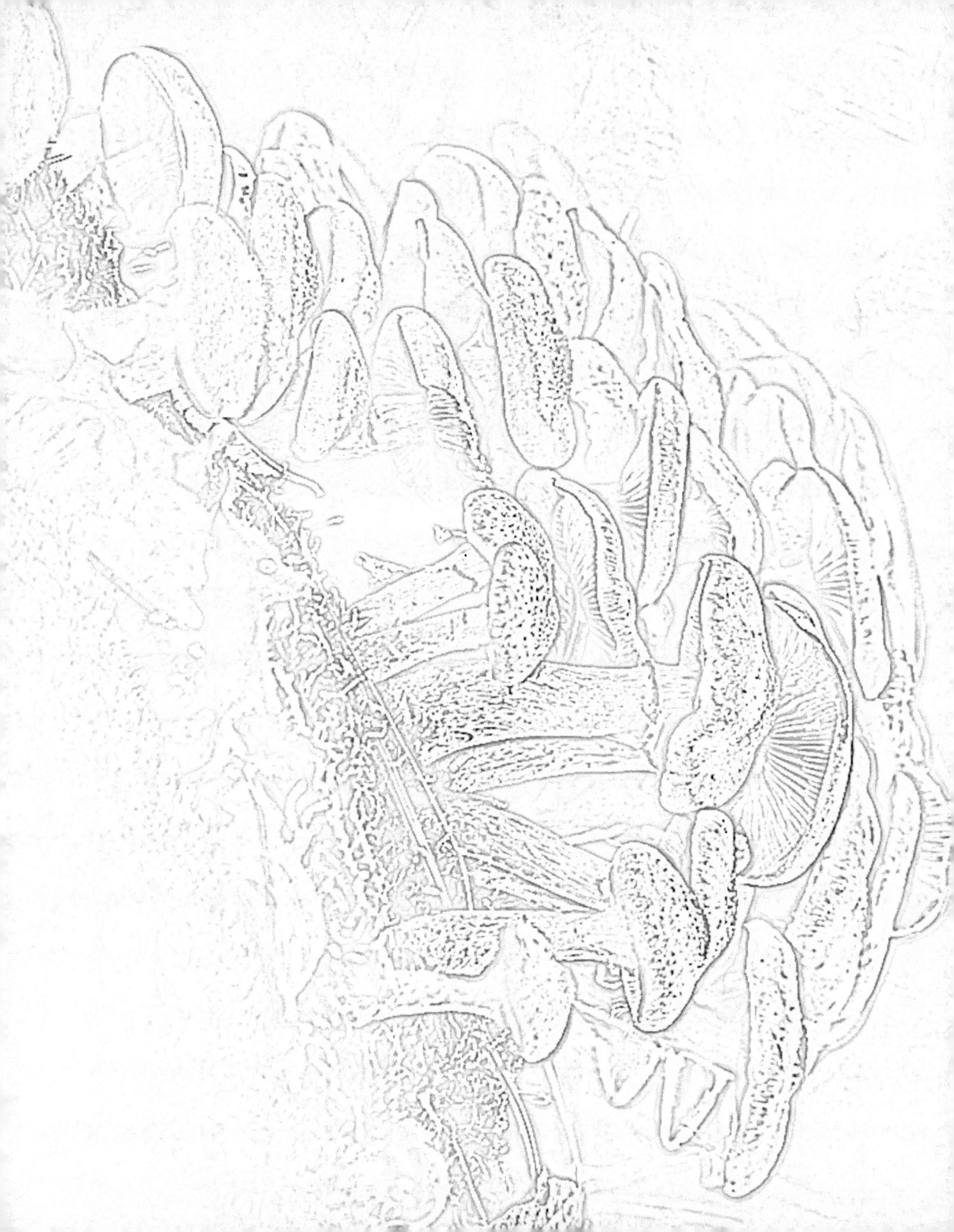

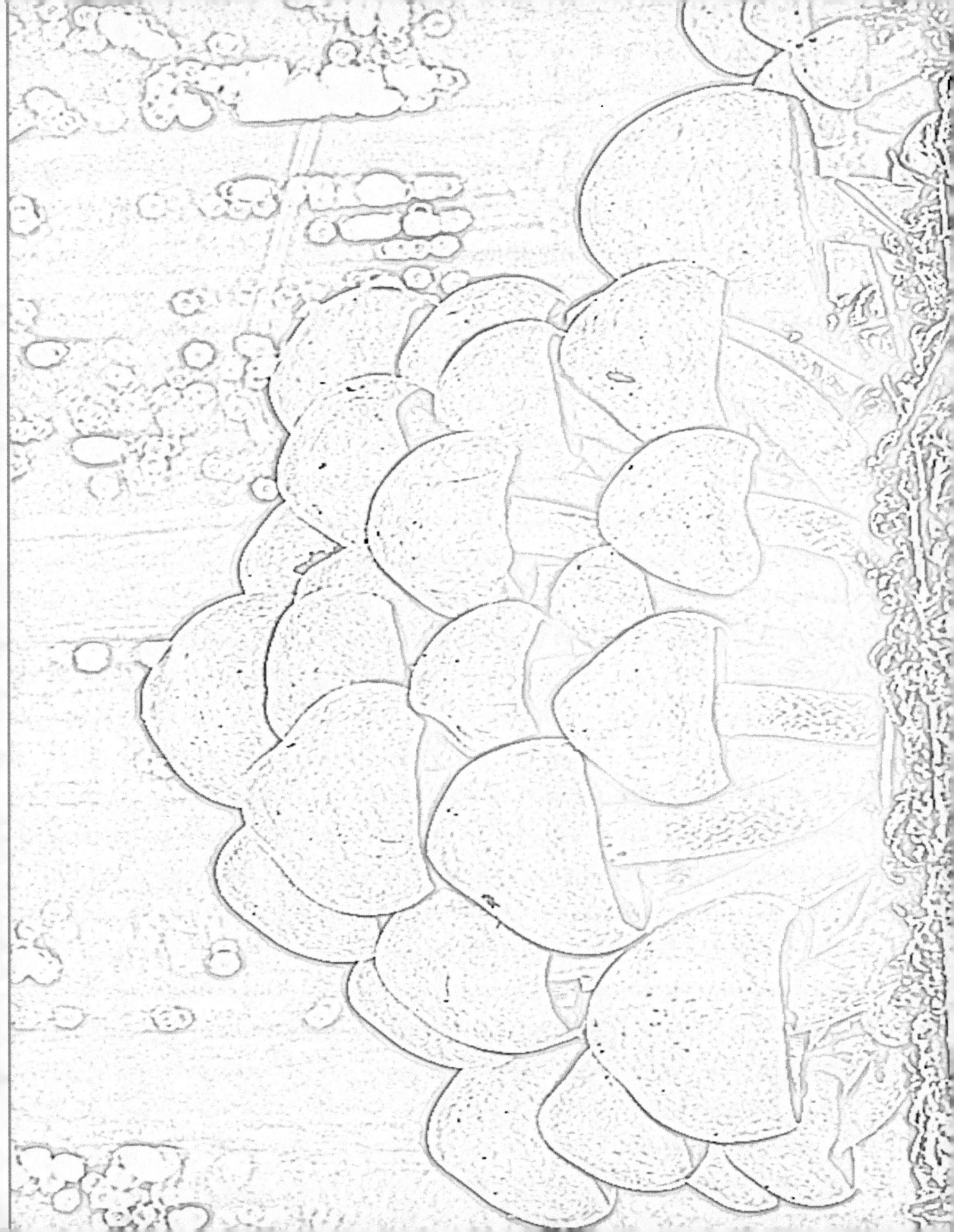

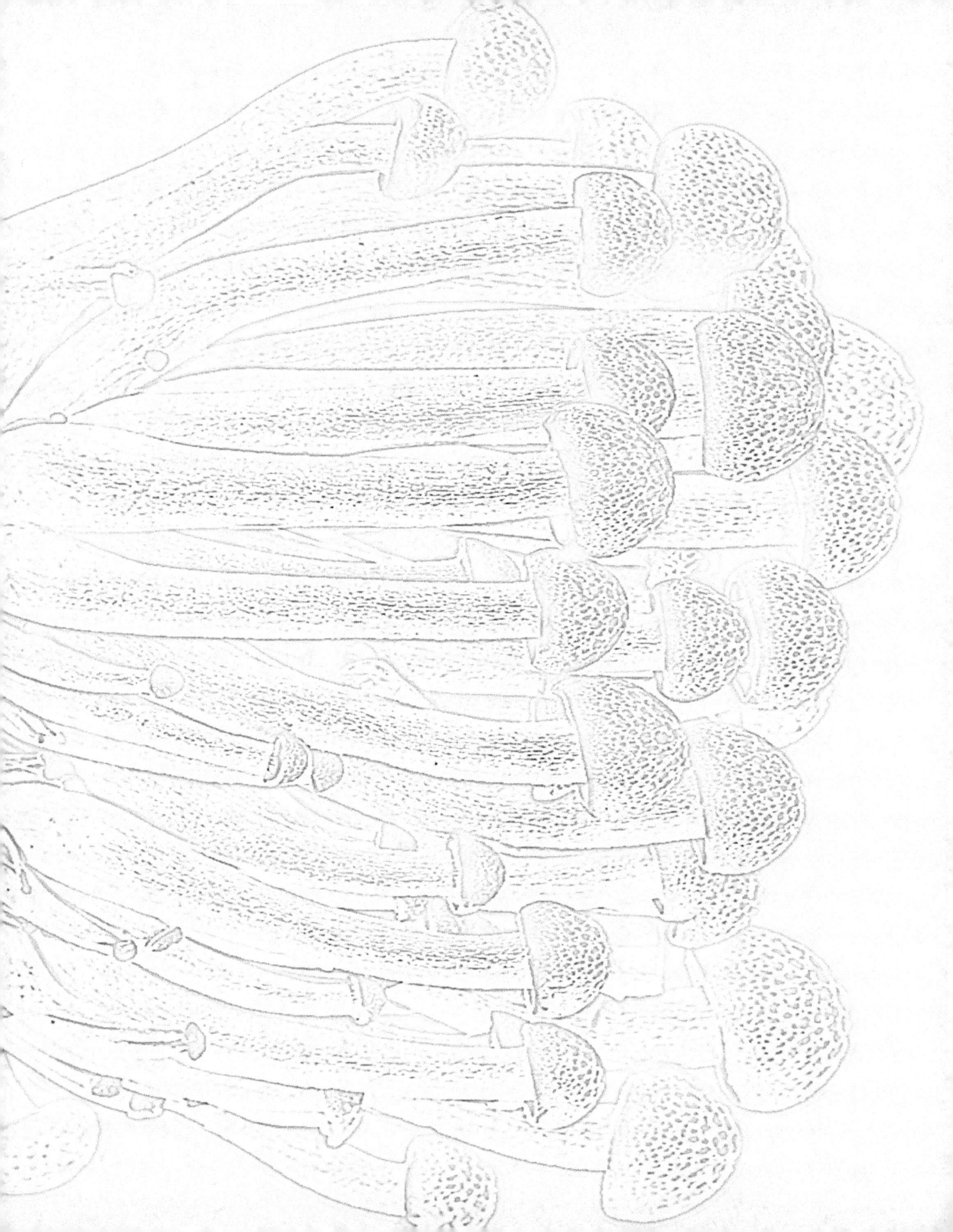

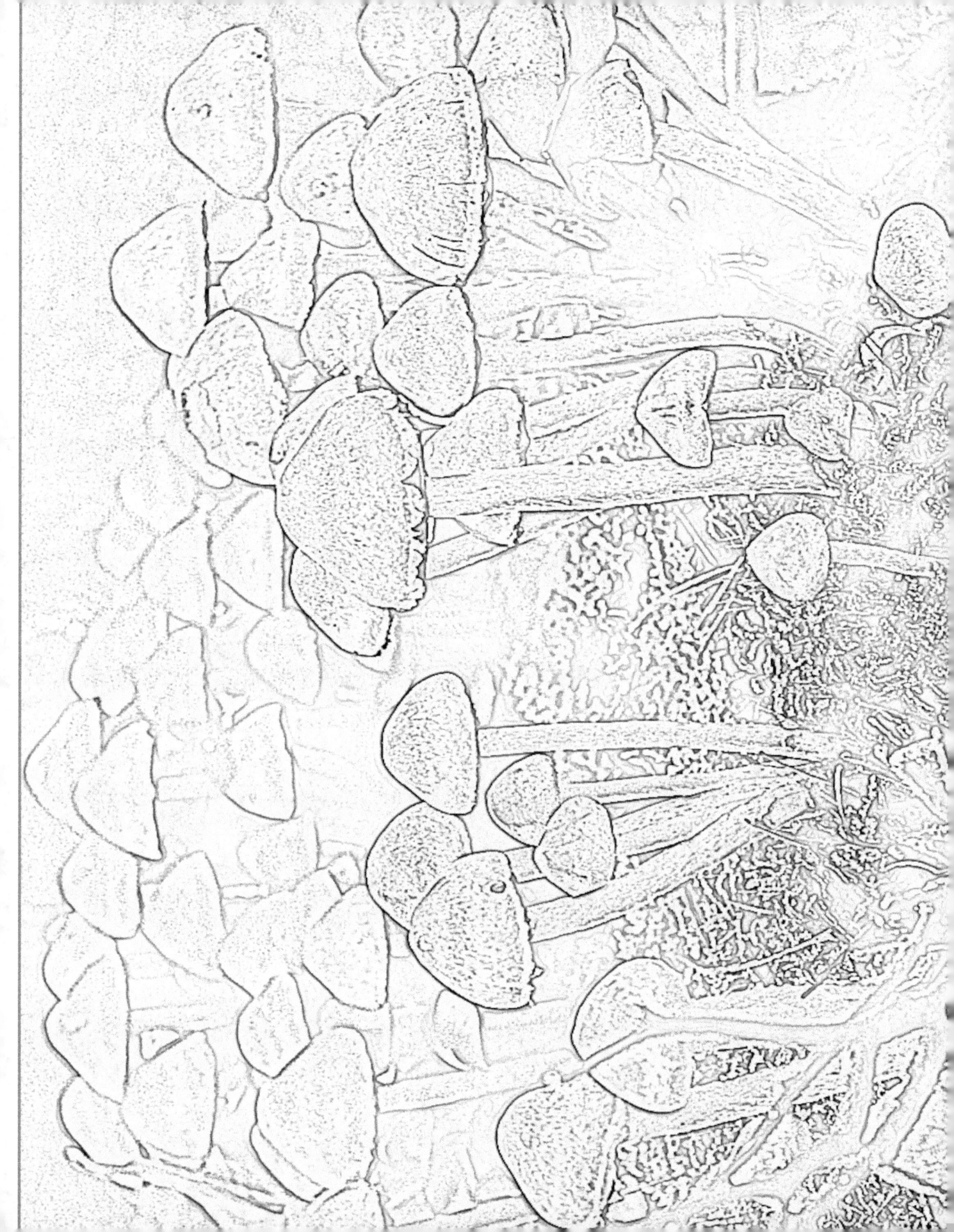

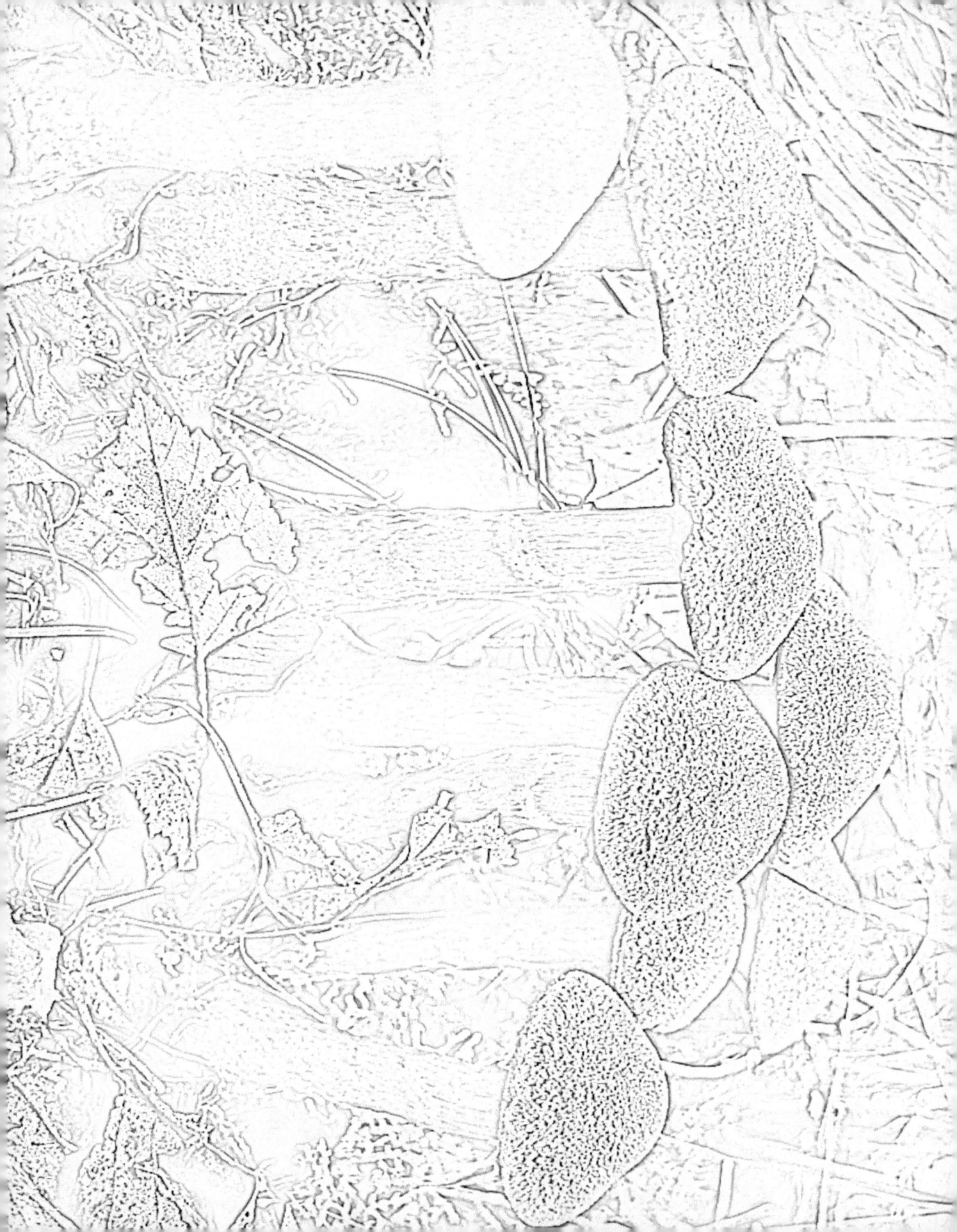

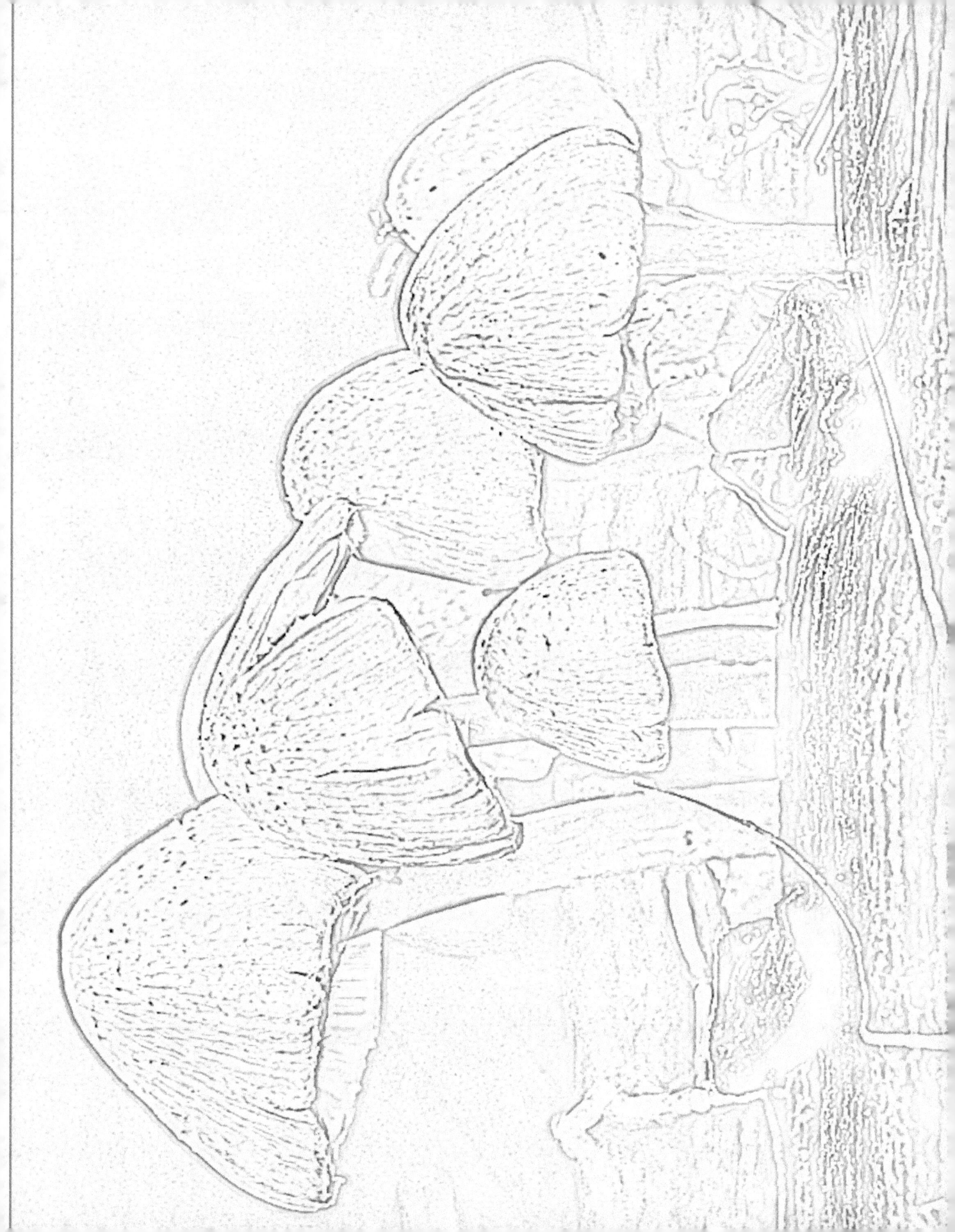

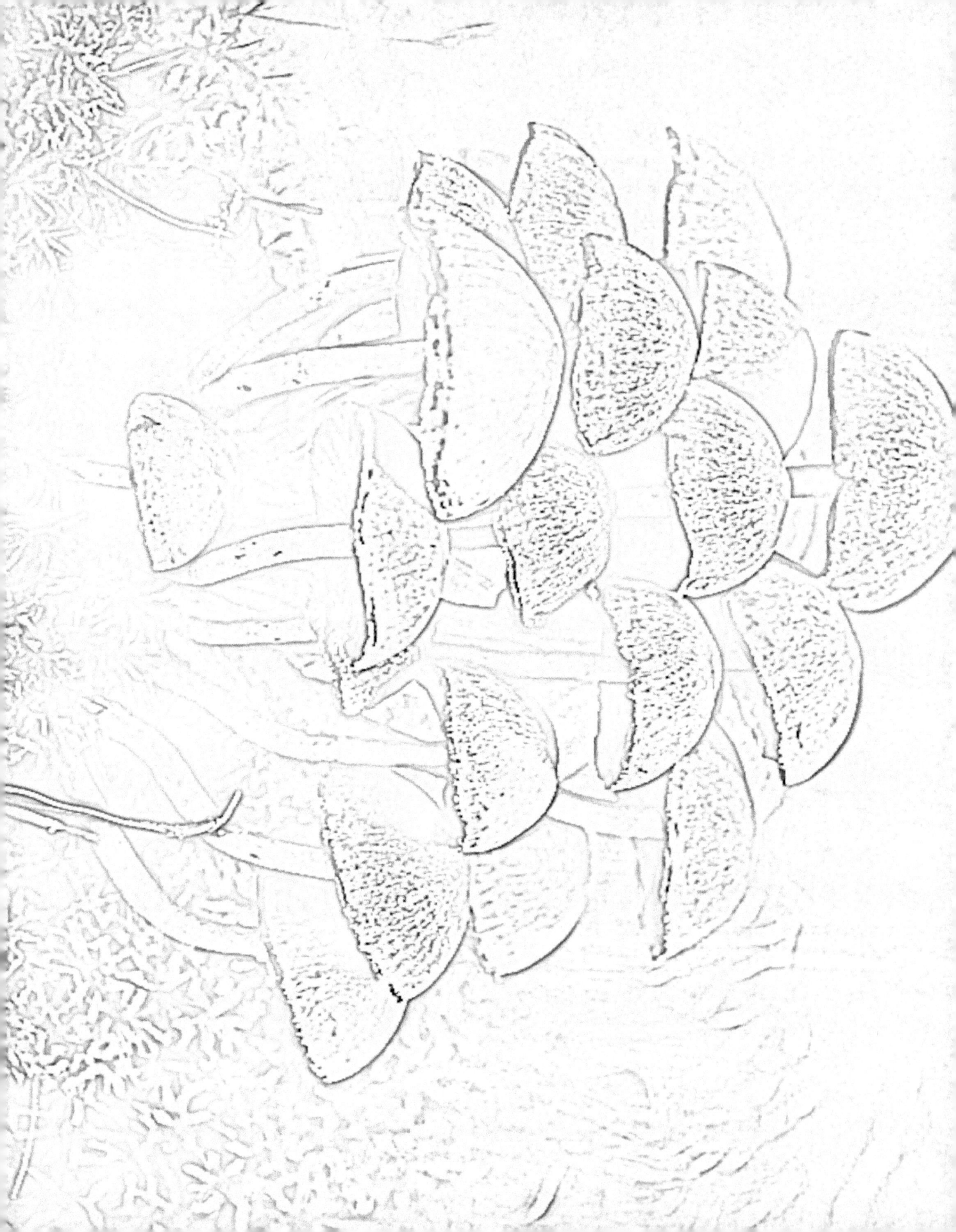

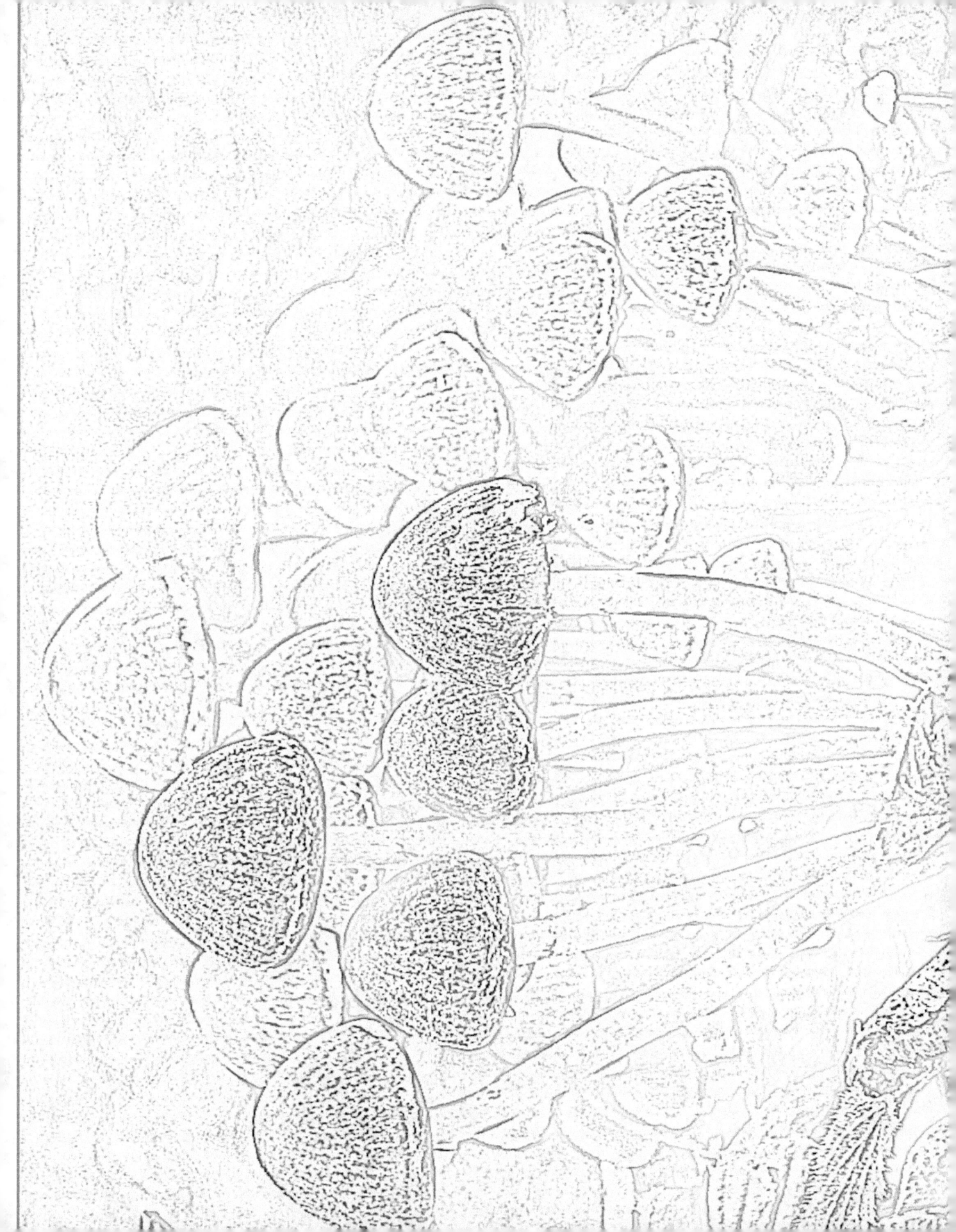

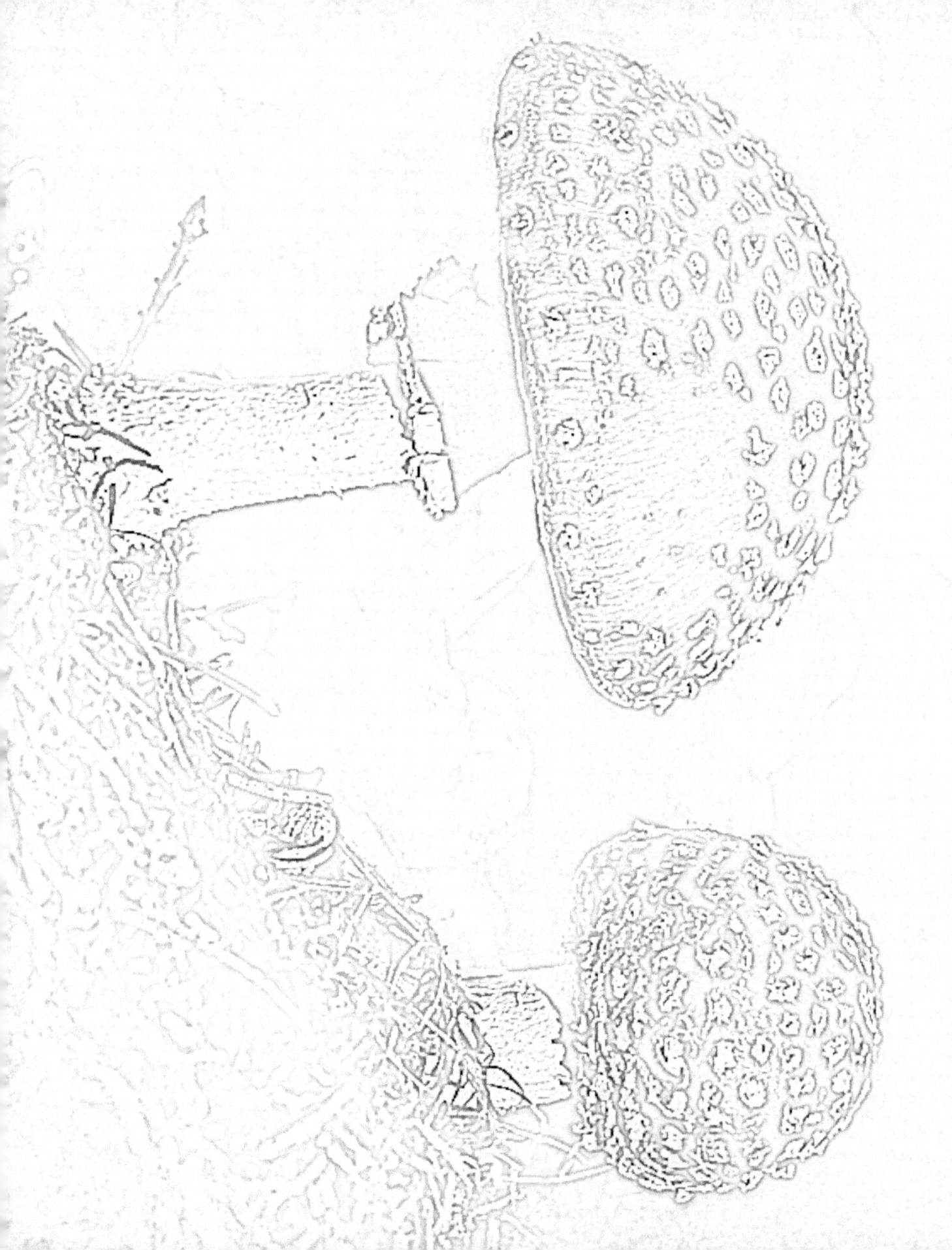

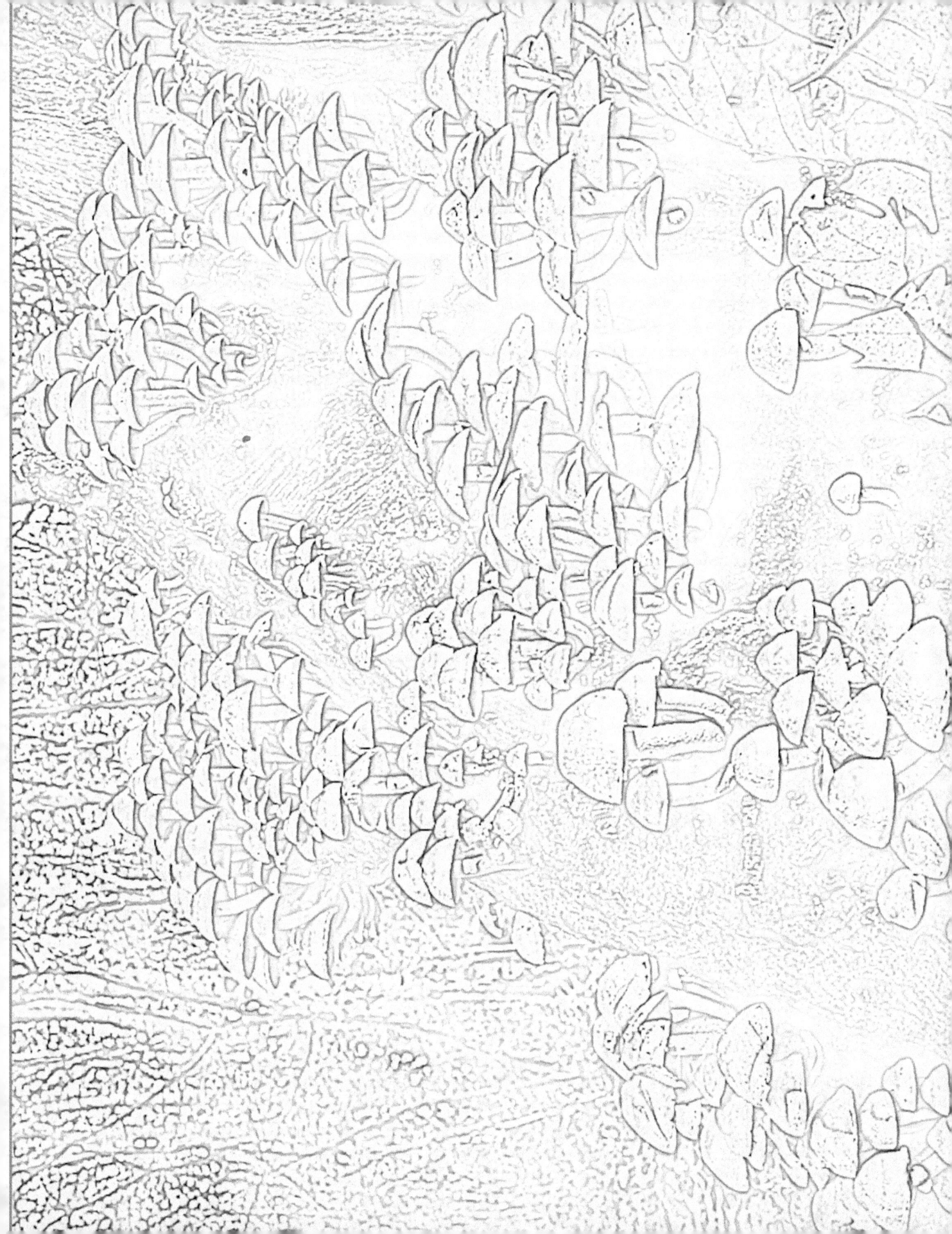

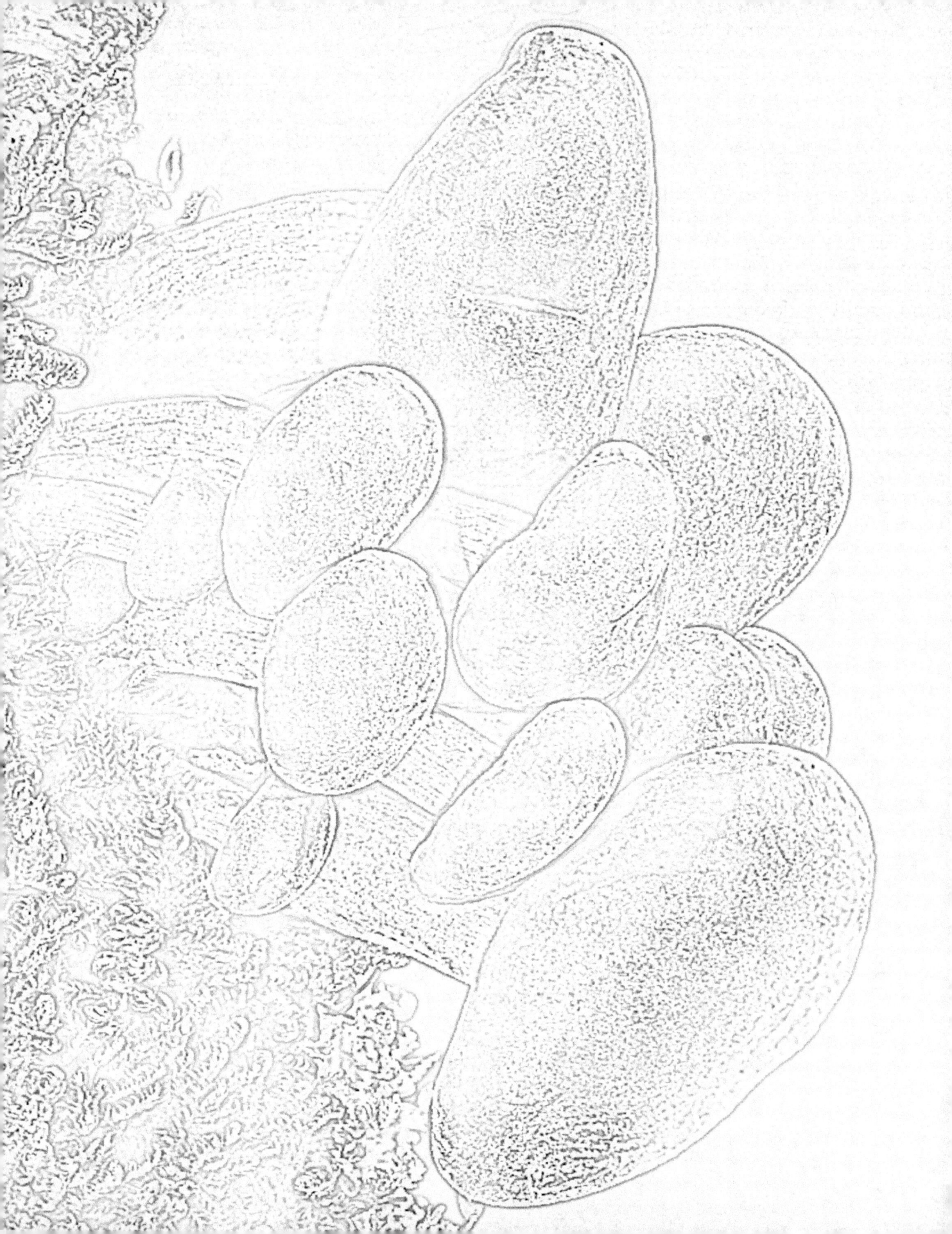

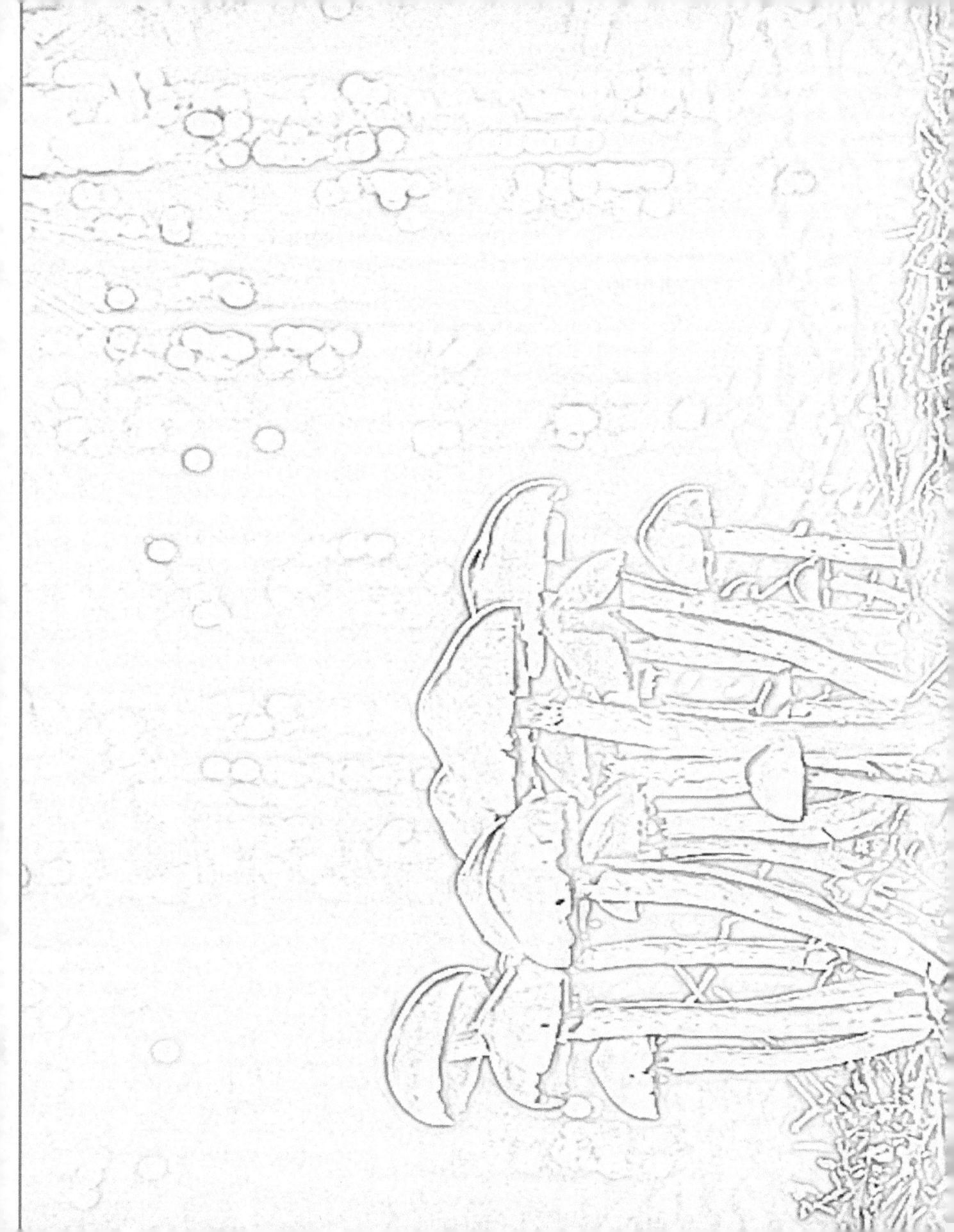

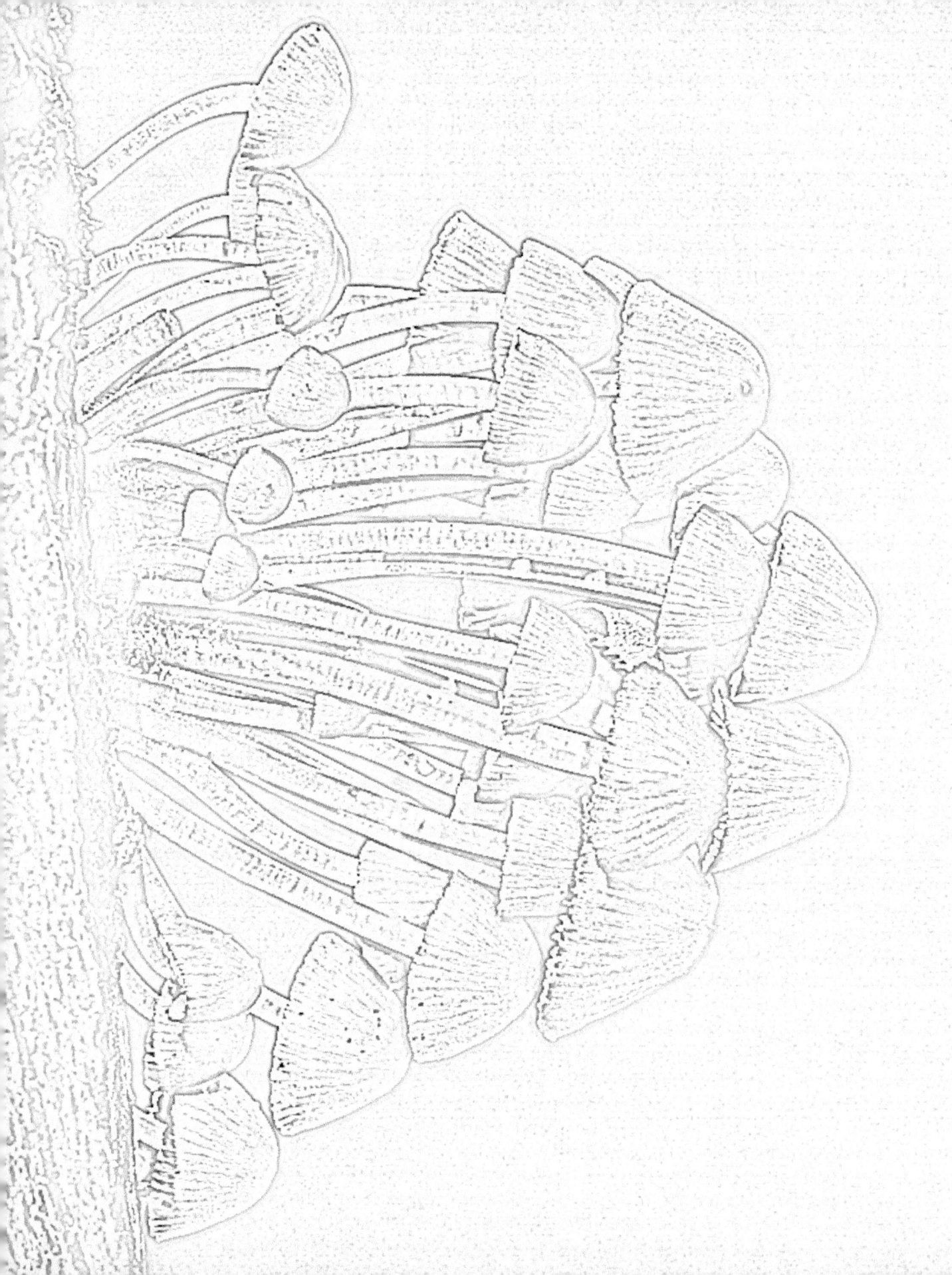

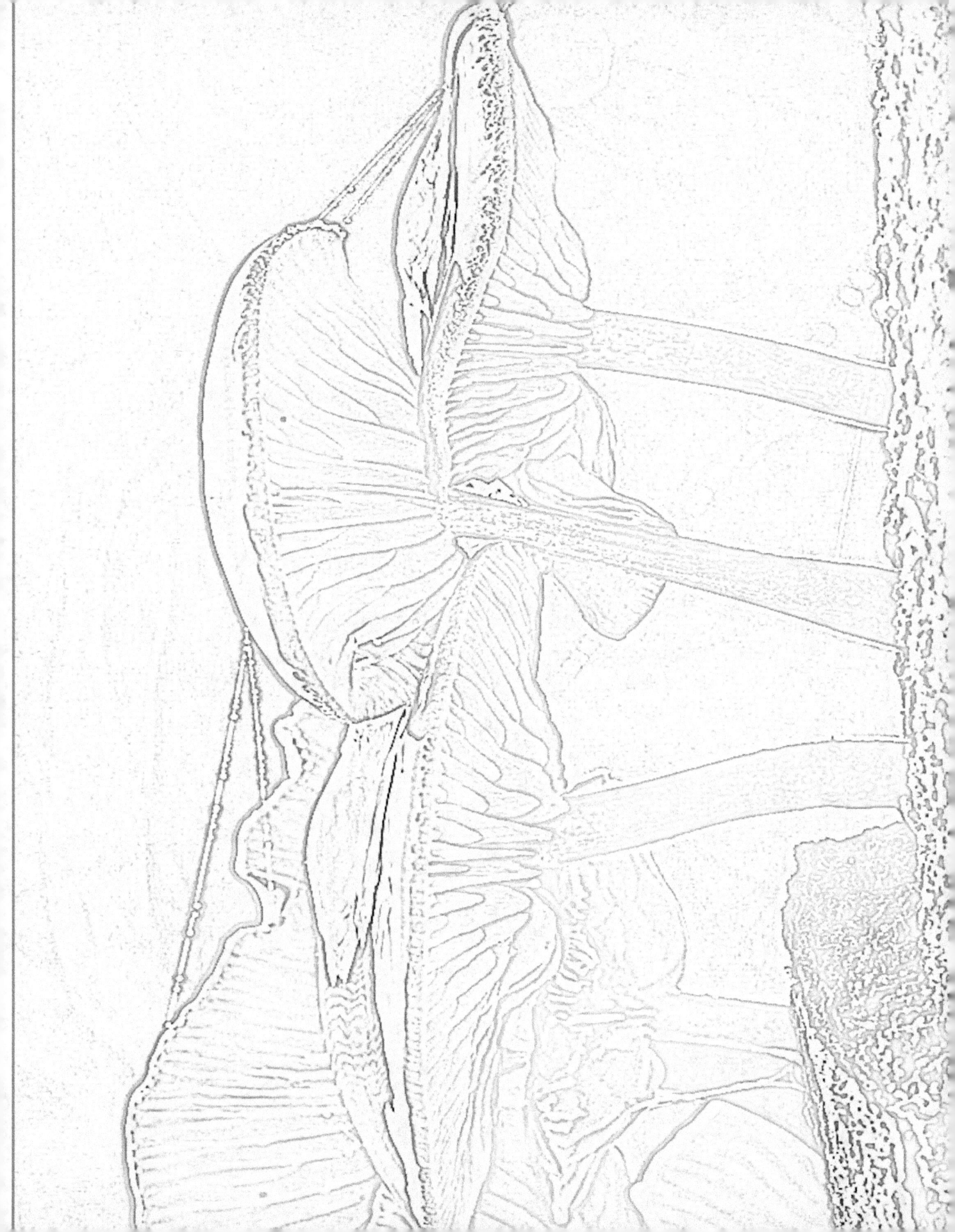

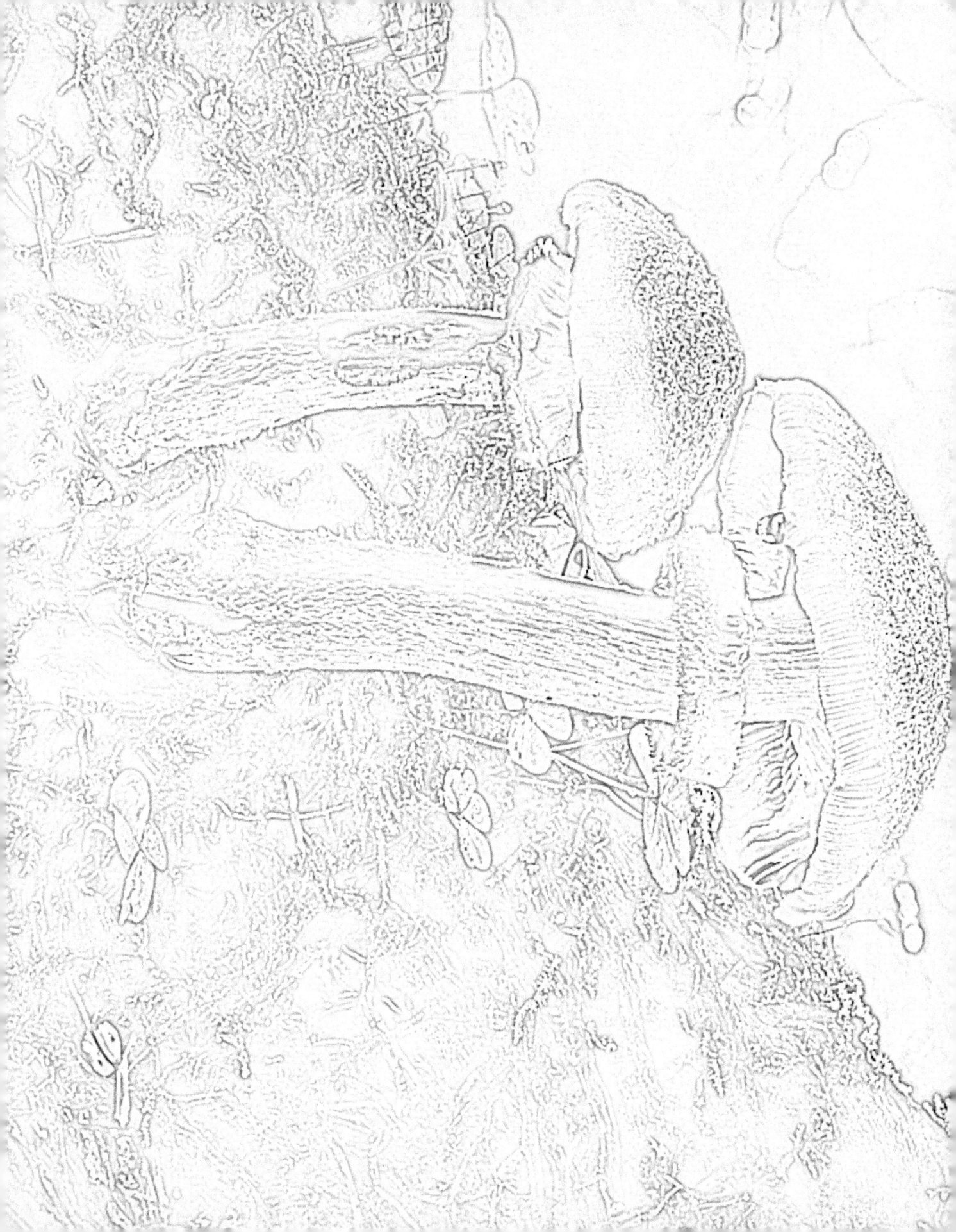

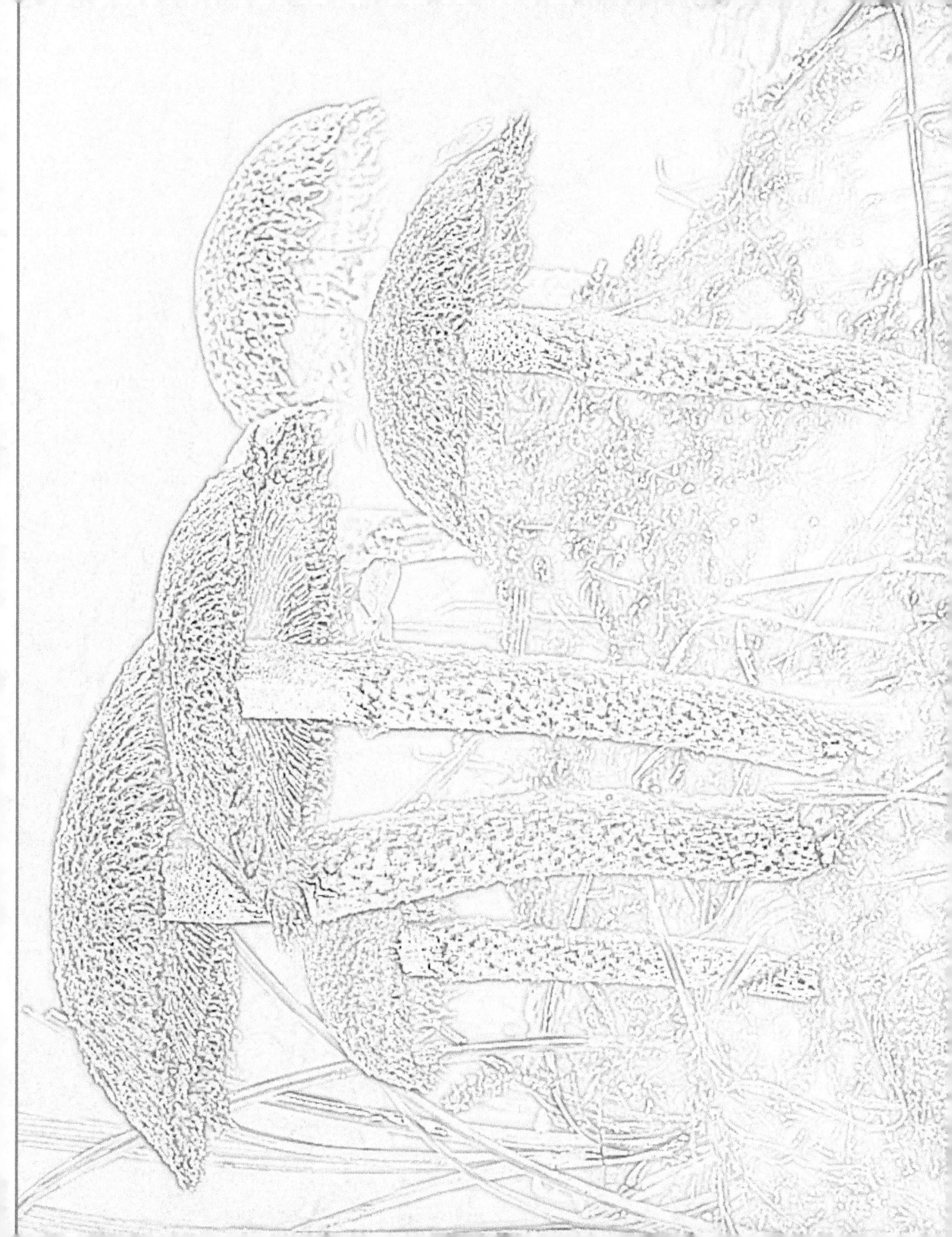

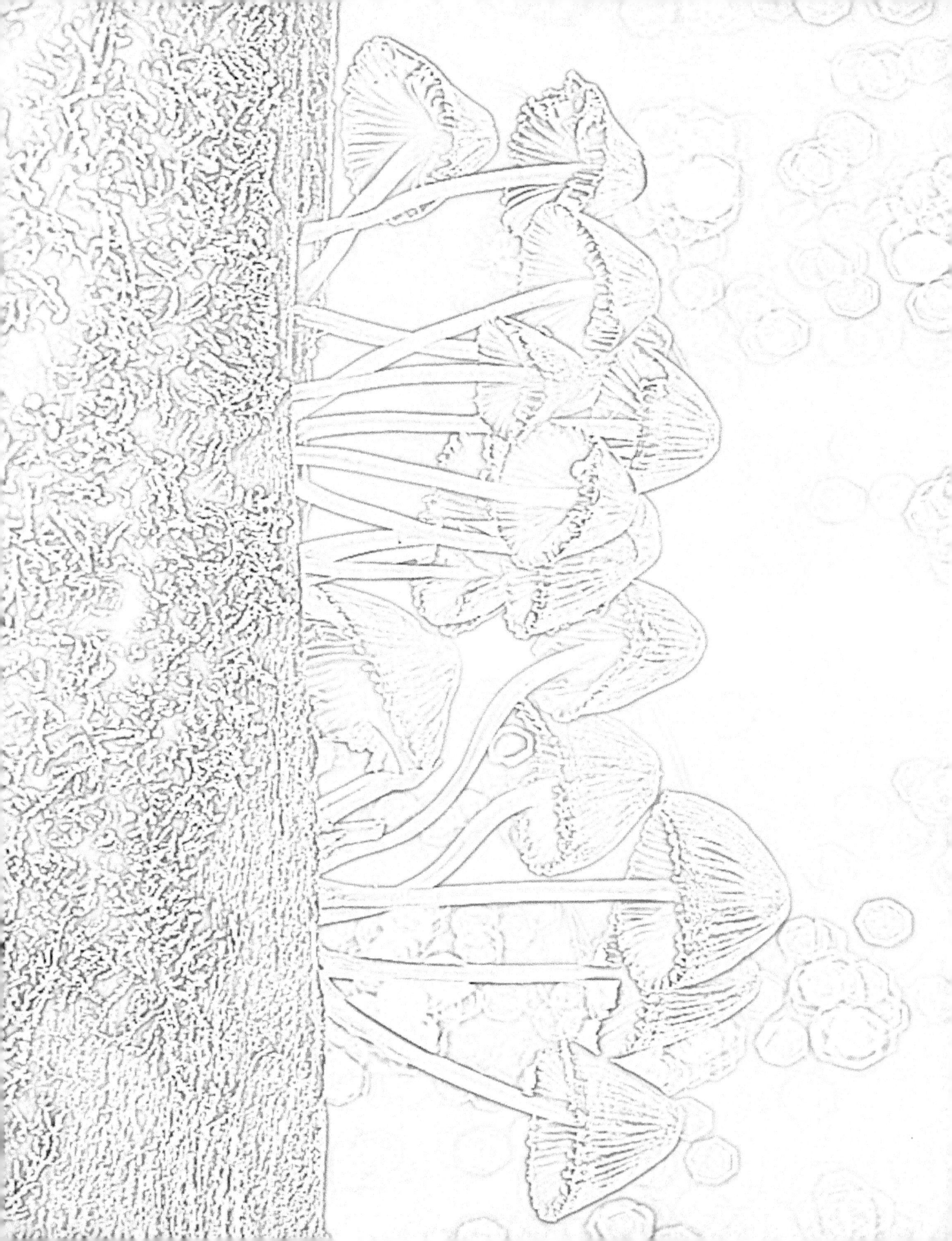

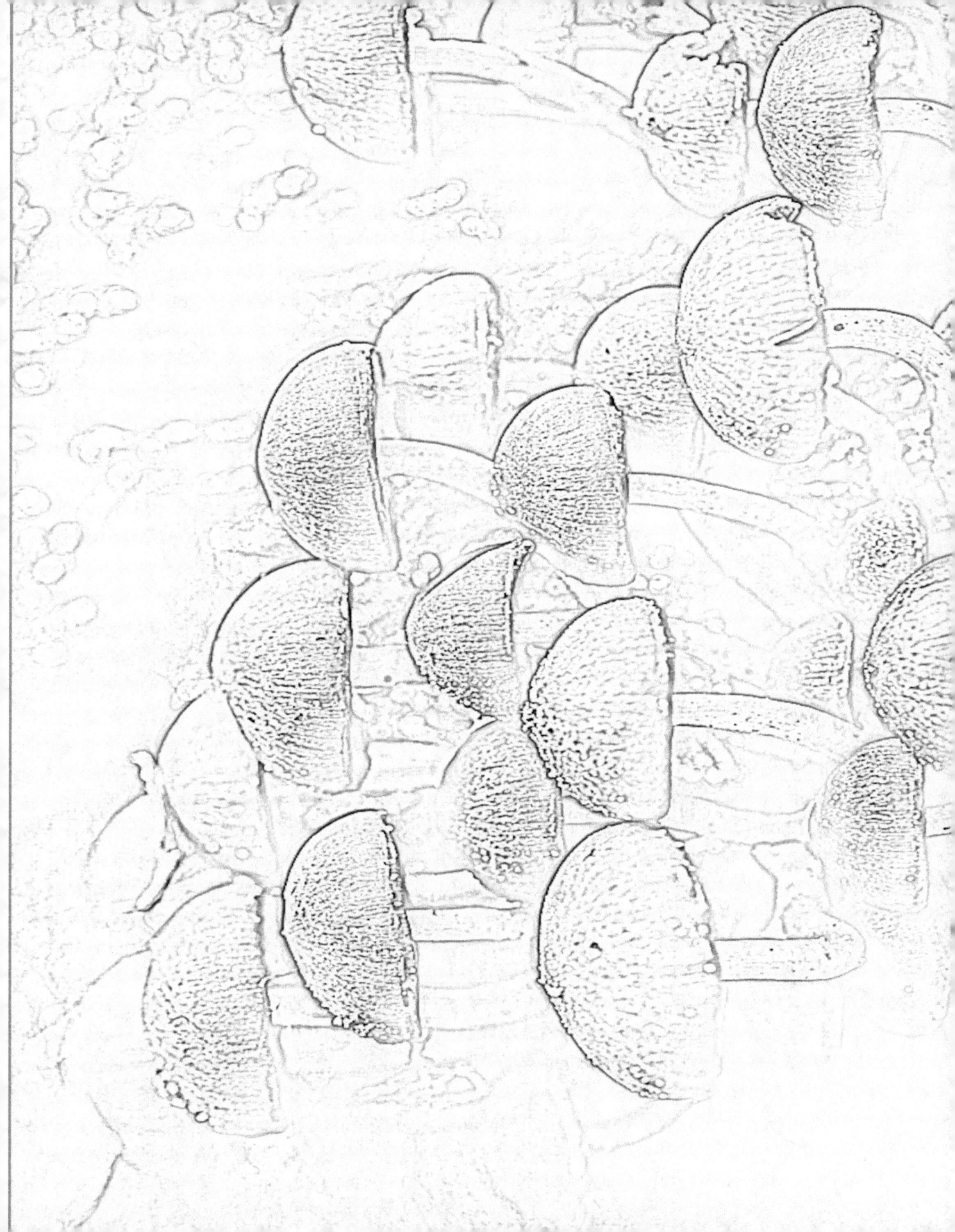

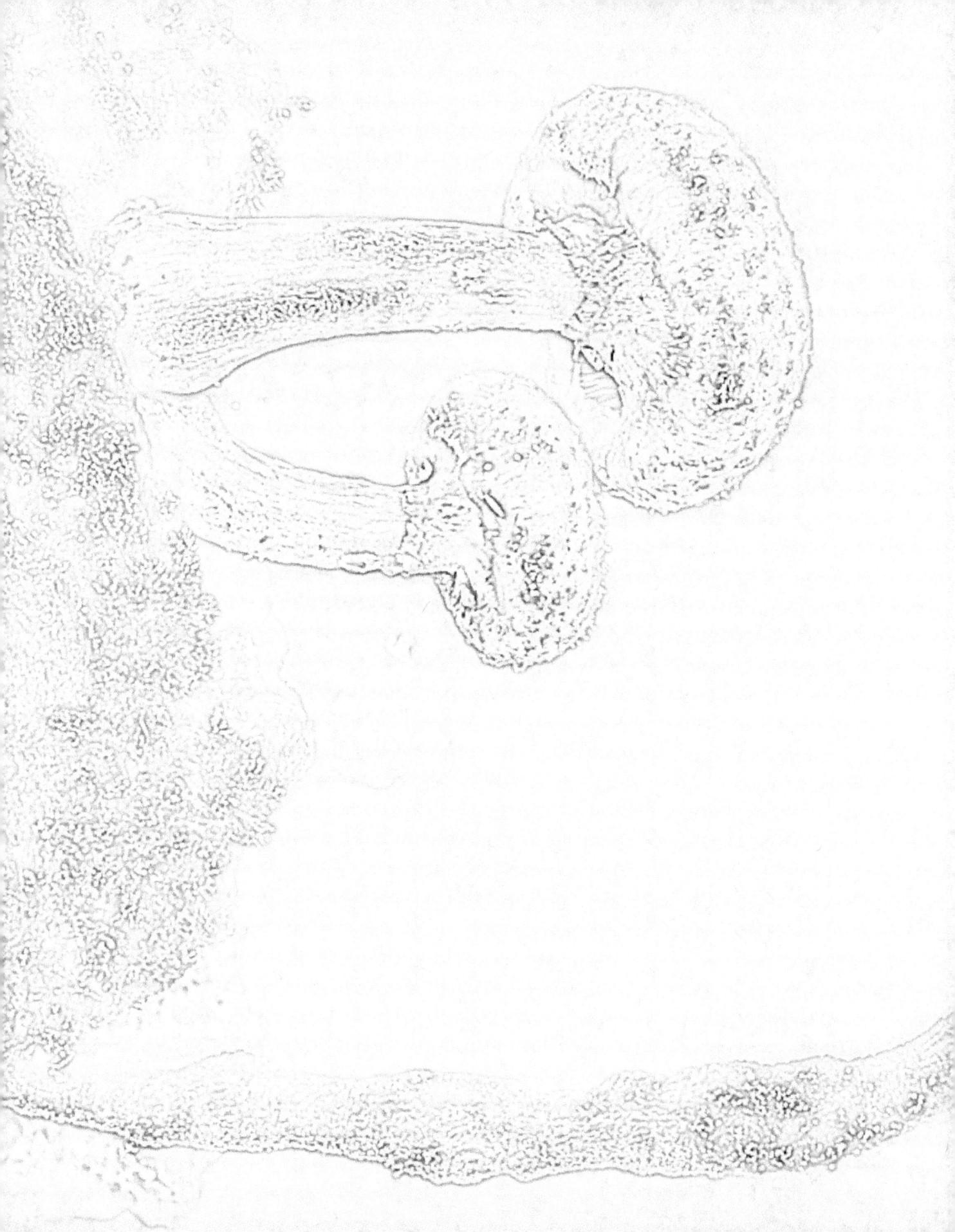

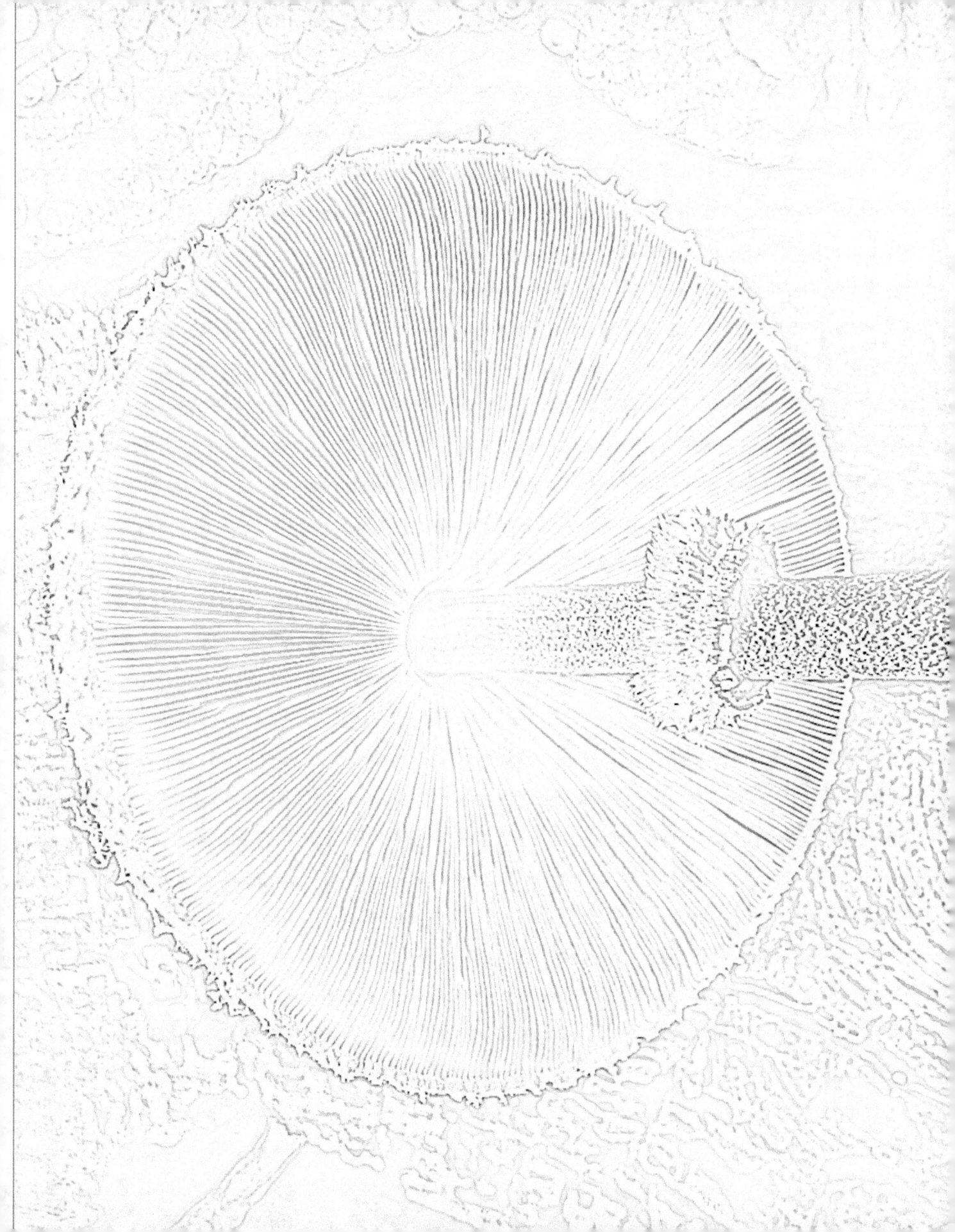

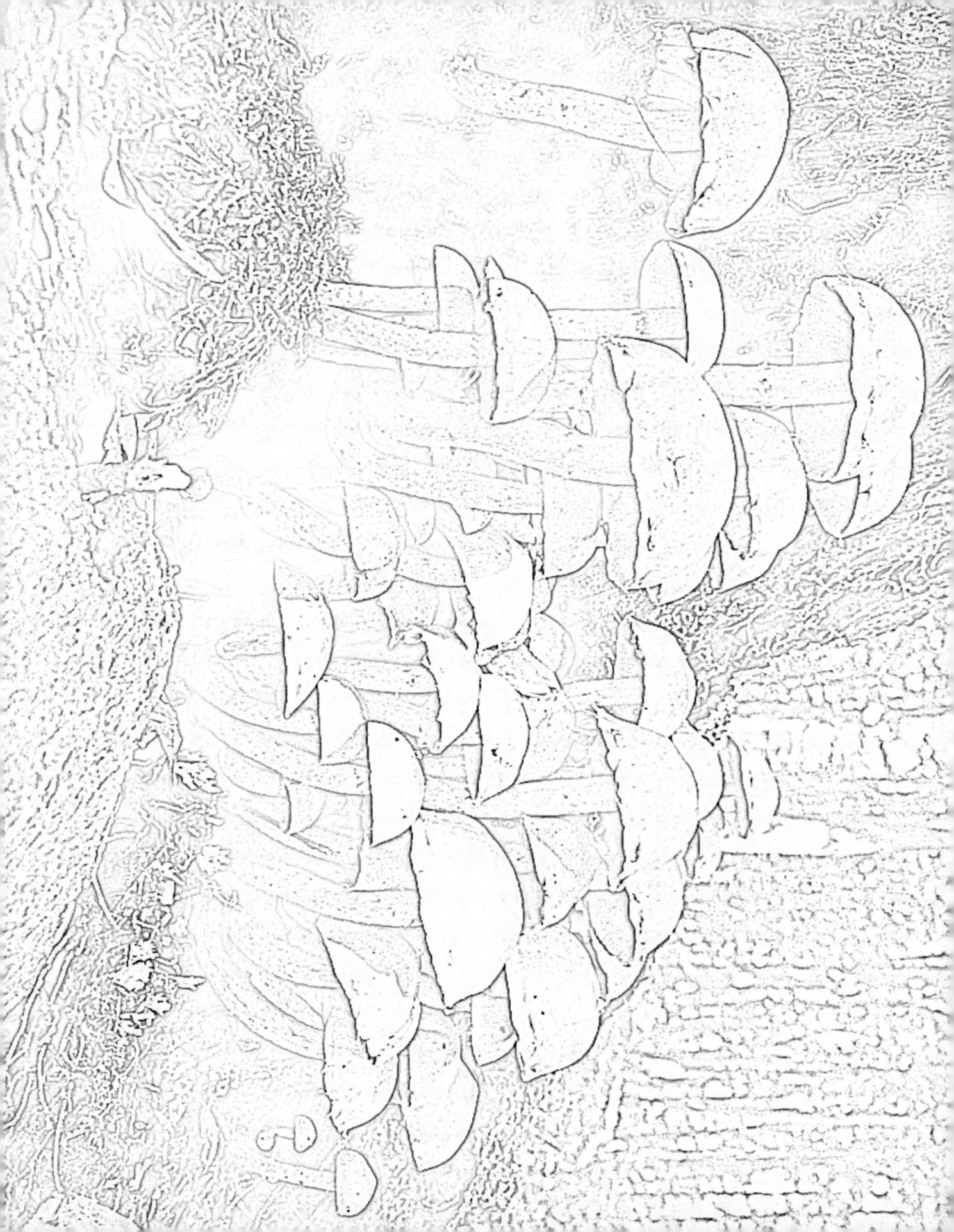

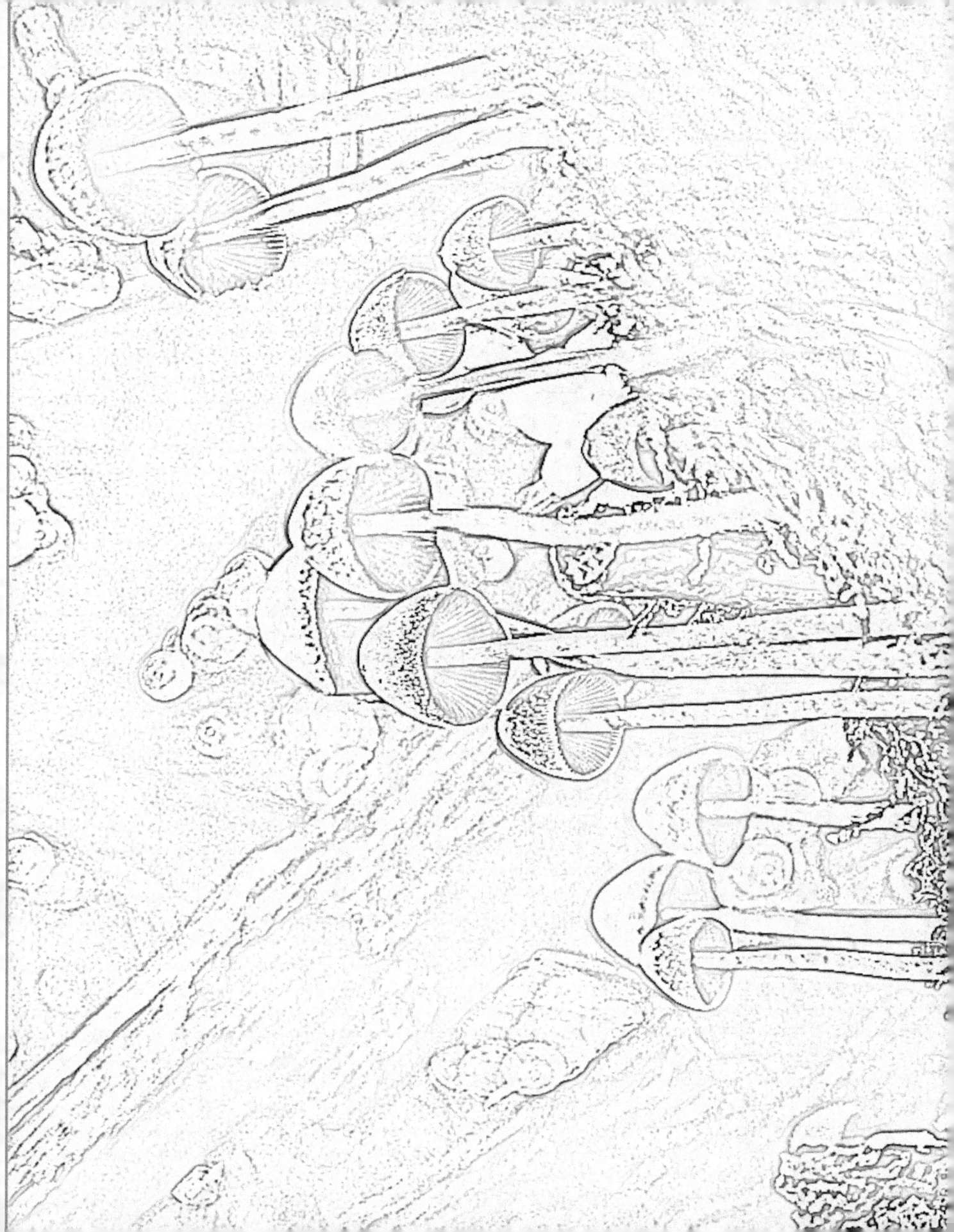

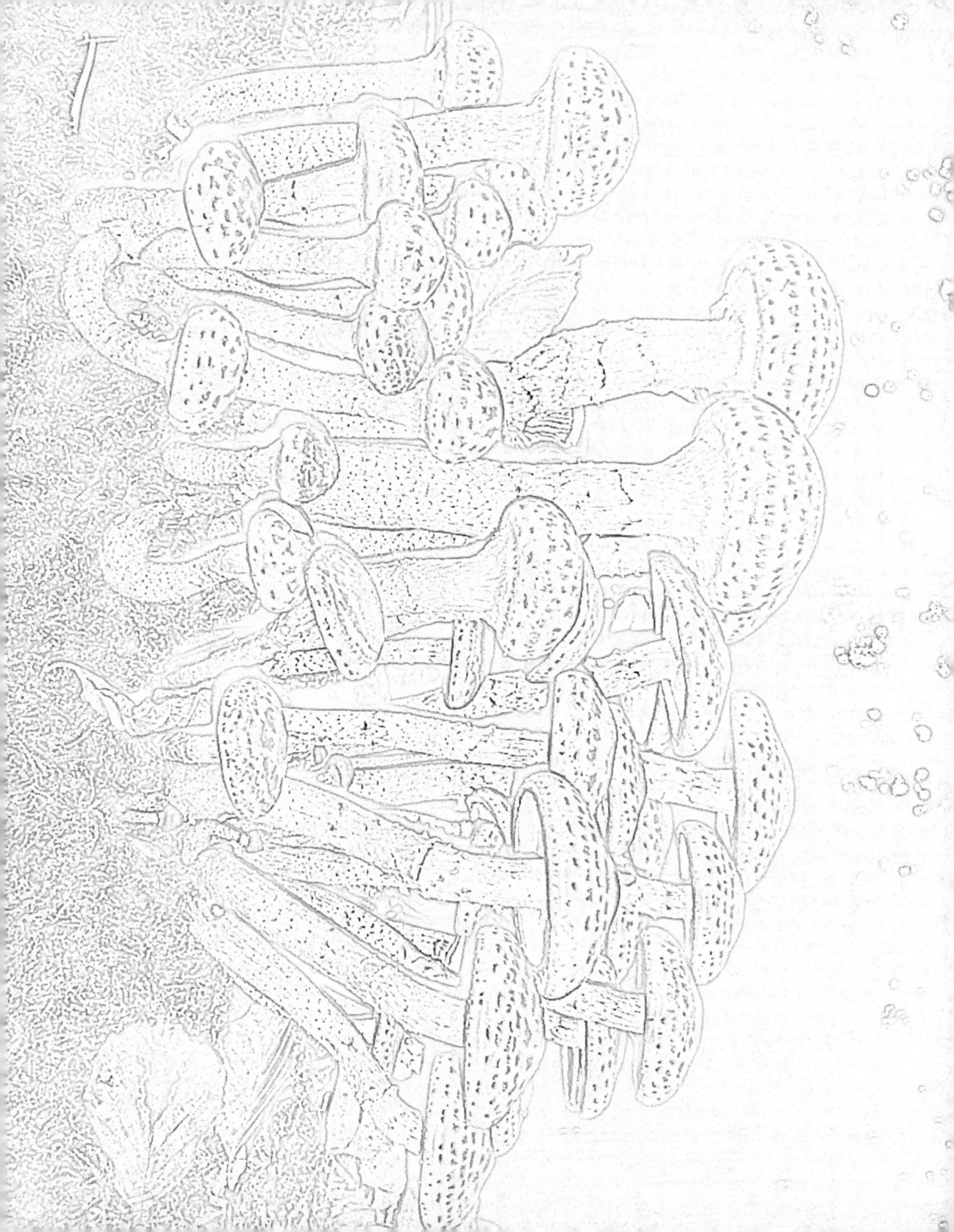

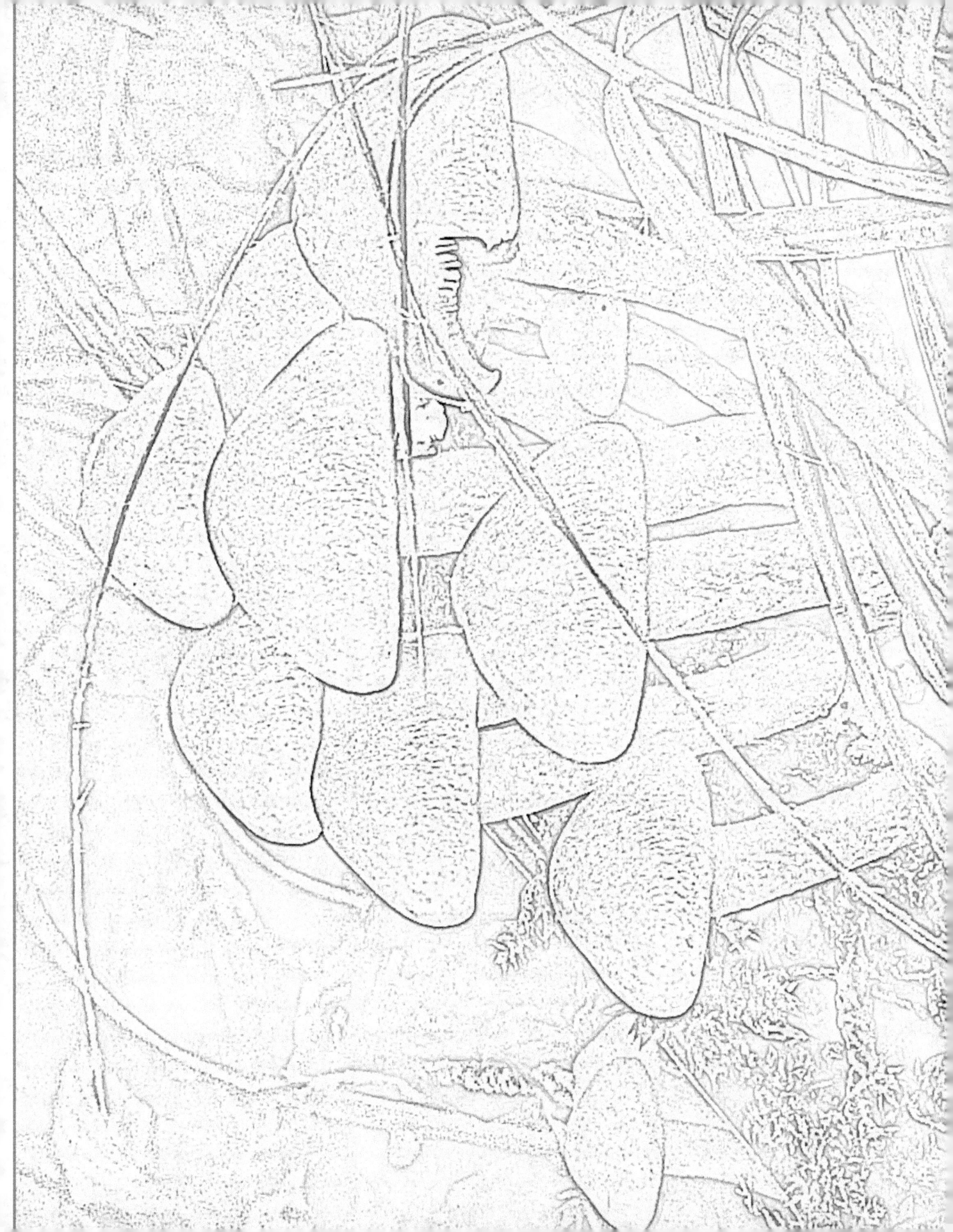

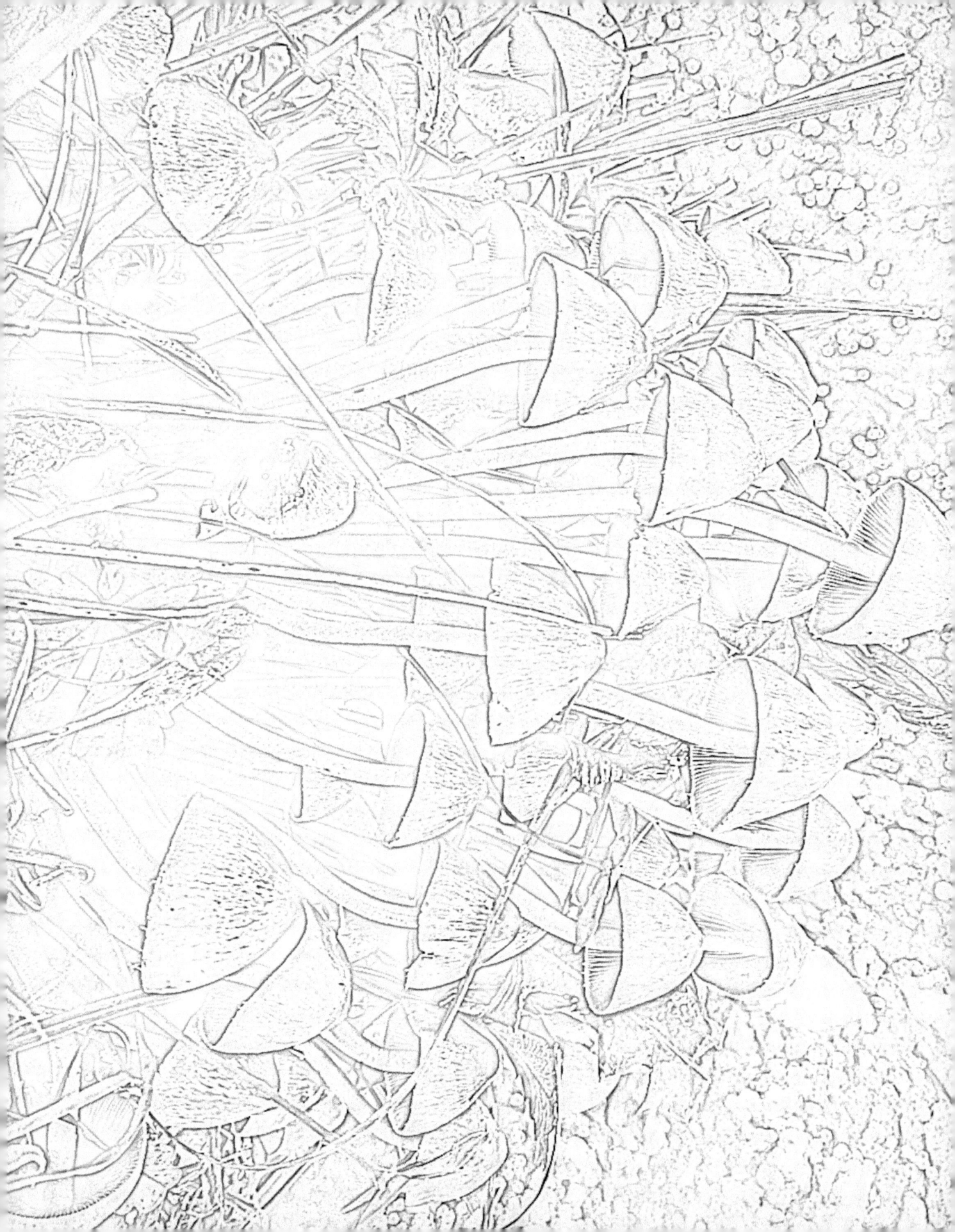

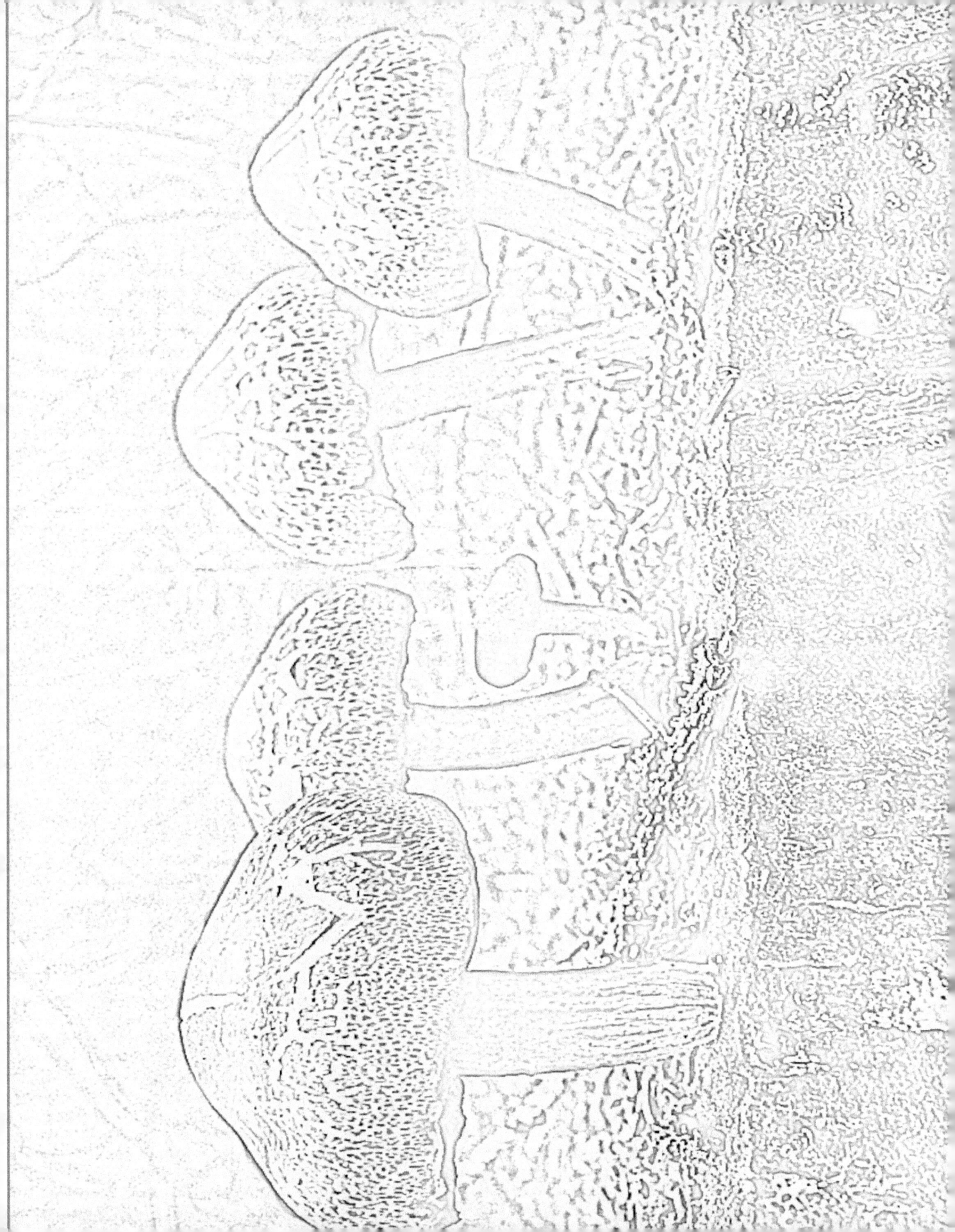

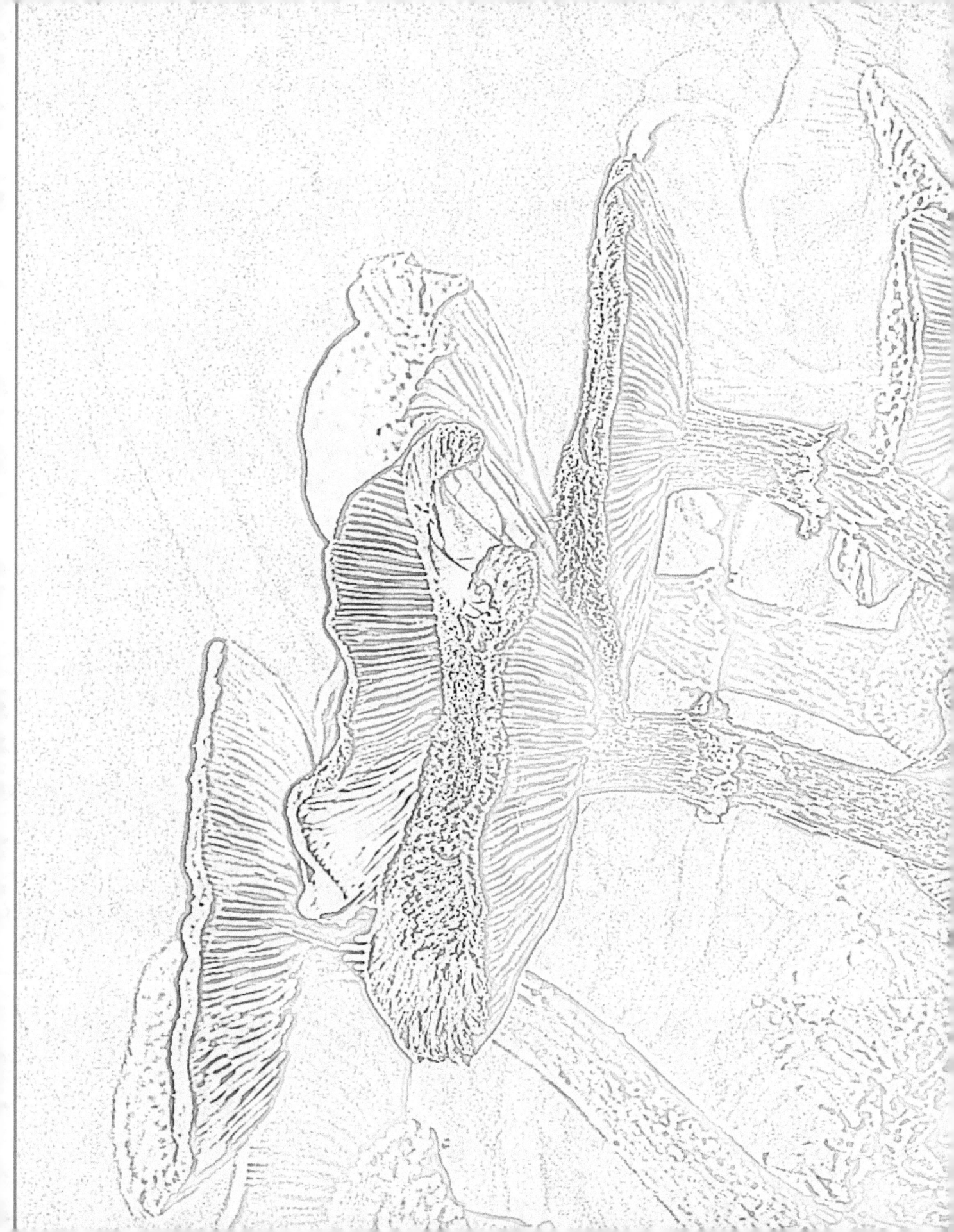

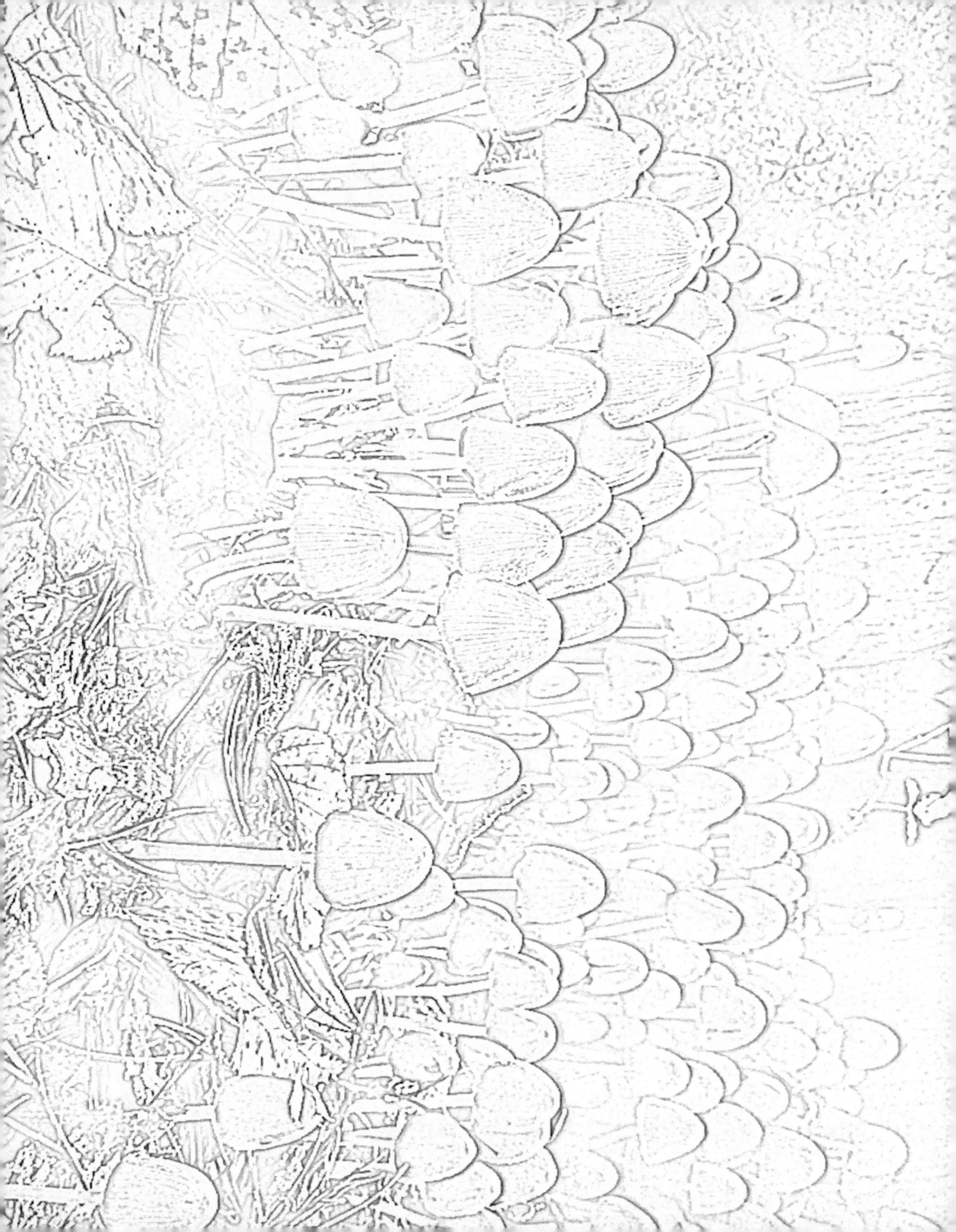

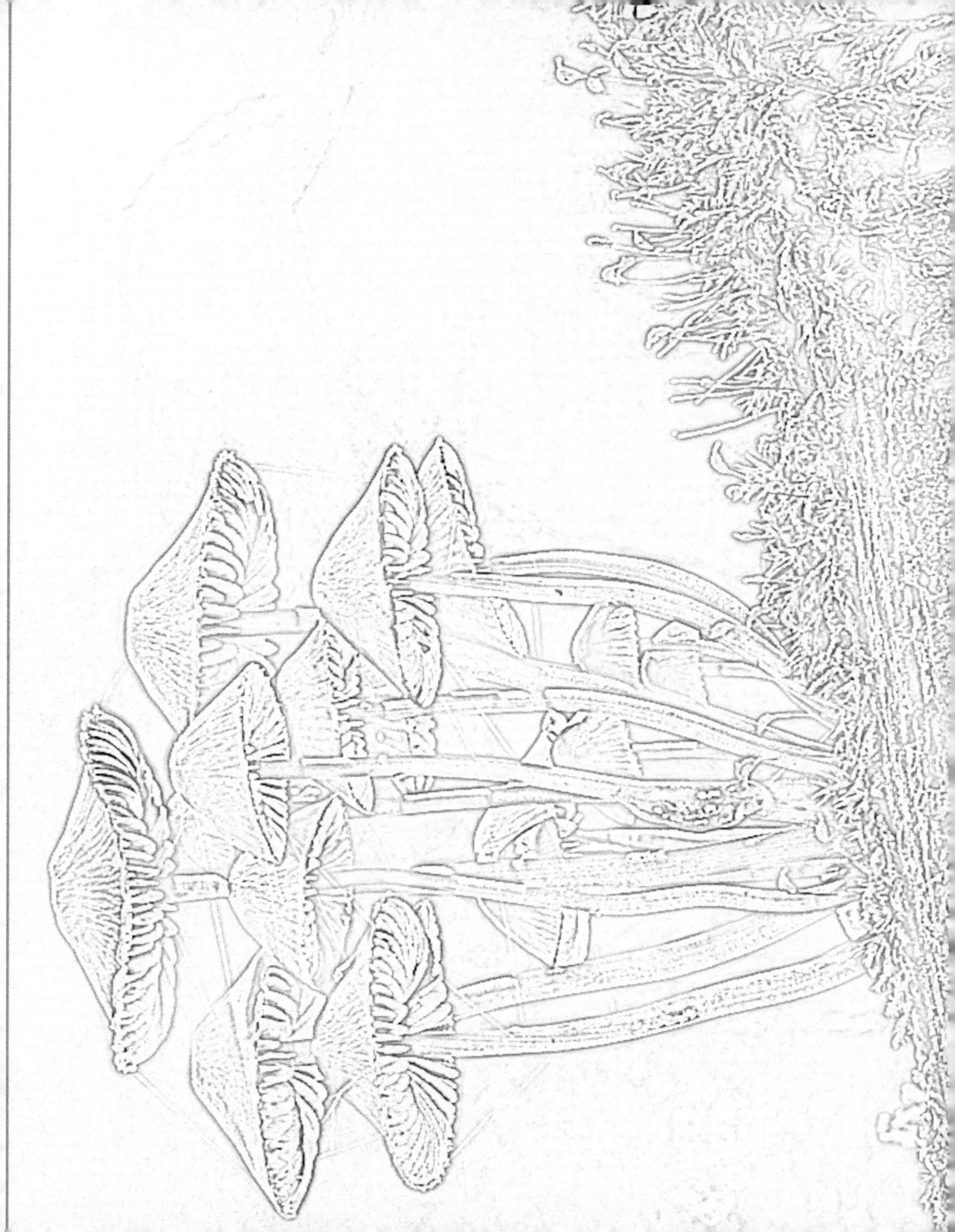